The Philosophy of Surrealism

the philosophy of Surrealism

Ferdinand Alquié

Translated by Bernard Waldrop

Ann Arbor

The University of Michigan Press

Copyright © by The University of Michigan 1965
All rights reserved
Library of Congress Catalog Card No. 65-20352
Published in the United States of America by
The University of Michigan Press and simultaneously
in Toronto, Canada, by Ambassador Books Limited
Manufactured in the United States of America
Originally published as Philosophie du surréalisme in 1955.

To the memory of Joë BOUSQUET
and Pierre SIRE,
and to my friend René NELLI,
who taught me that poetry is also truth.

Contents

Introduction

We readily reproach the author of a book for not having treated a subject he has not chosen. Readers do not care what he wants them to hear; it is their own project, their own wants they are interested in. So I must give notice at the start that this is not a history of surrealism, such as the work of M. Nadeau,[1] who presents that history with the support of many useful documents, or those *Entretiens* in which André Breton traces—this time from within—his spiritual adventure and that of the movement he inspired. Neither have I attempted a study of the sources of surrealism. It has, of course, its origins, and these may be pursued both in the works approved and admired by the surrealists and in the writings they oppose, writings whose affirmations they invert. Still, an author approves an idea or opposes a tendency only in the name of internal demands which, before he chooses at all, make him what he is; it is these demands and their essential goals that I have taken as my starting point for understanding surrealism. It seems to me they alone make it possible to assess what in surrealism is unique and irreplaceable. I have further excluded the techniques of surrealism and what one could call its aesthetic or its poetics. No doubt some will claim that I have thereby neglected the main point. But those interested in these problems can write about them. My only matter here is the philosophy of surrealism.

Philosophy of surrealism does not, moreover, mean surrealist philosophy. One could object too easily that the surrealists are not philosophers in the strict sense: they express themselves essentially in poetry and painting. And our age is no doubt only too drawn to confusing philosophy and art. But it also confuses without trouble philosophy and the sciences. To distinguish philosophy from science we must realize that philosophy is an undertaking of man as a whole, not a system concerning objects. It is beyond question that, in this sense, surrealist research has something at once nonliterary and nonscientific and that it aims at observing and exploring regions neglected by physics as well as by the arts; its procedures are as little reducible to rational methods as to strictly aesthetic expression. Besides, surrealism involves an authentic theory of love, of life, of the imagination, of the relations between man and the world. All this supposes a philosophy, which I have tried to isolate and define. Thus, no one should be surprised if, without limiting myself to him, I have paid particular attention to André Breton, who has been—even more than its leader—the surrealist movement's intellectual and reflective consciousness. I regret not giving to others all the space that in different areas they deserve and not determining what Breton himself owes to them; I am aware that surrealism was not the child of André Breton alone and that he himself has claimed not to create and define surrealist truth but to expound it and be faithful to it. Even so, in his work this truth attains greatest clarity.

Moreover, even the definition of surrealism would become unwieldy if distinguished from Breton's expressed ideas taken as a whole. To ask who really has or has not been surrealist would end in insoluble quarrels over words—any reference to a surrealism *an sich* being naturally impossible. As those splitting with Breton have generally ceased to call themselves surrealists, we can consider Breton's thought as essence and norm for the philosophy of surrealism without wronging anyone. The ideas of each of those no longer in the surrealist "group" would likewise require separate studies. It would be very interesting to decide what the conceptions of Salvador Dali or Miró owe or do not owe to surrealism. There is a surrealist humor in Raymond Queneau, a surrealist fantasy in Jacques Prévert. Furthermore, surrealist beauty may be found in works of authors having no connection with the surrealist movement: the atmosphere of Kafka's stories, strange, quasi-supernatural, and so uneasily explained by their author's conscious intents, is on more than one count comparable to the atmosphere of surrealism. And the emotion struck in us by the stunning chapter of "The Two Letters" in Yassu Gauclère's *La Clé* is that of encounters and of objective chance.[2] I could not hope to extend this examination to so many questions.

This is not then, in any degree, a work of literary history. Surrealism is considered here in its effort toward the only truth. Breton has indeed spoken, at the beginning of the *Second Manifesto,* of "the absurd distinction between the beautiful and the ugly, the true and the false, good and evil." But he says also, in his *Enquête sur l'amour,* that the "pursuit of truth" is "at the base of any valuable activity," and his work is shot through by incessant appeals to morality, to beauty; Breton is indignant then at what is customarily called beautiful, true, good—only in the name of a beautiful, a true, a good that he judges more authentic. And if, in order to realize man, he rises against all dualisms, his fidelity to human experience, his sincerity, his lucidity lead him in many cases to recover truths that the dualistic philosophies brought to light. Finally, calling himself the enemy of metaphysics, Breton arrives often—by his own ways —at truths taught by metaphysics; for surrealism, anxious for total liberation, never accepts wholly the idea that consciousness has become unhappy in time and may therefore escape from its unhappiness. Though it harps on social alienation and hopes for salvation in the future, surrealism sees also that the unhappiness of consciousness is not linked only to its history, but to its eternal condition. Thus, on many points, its consciousness of man leads it to recover the spirit of metaphysics and in any case to oppose the current of an epoch in which no one is any longer concerned with the essential absence, in which each man measures his hope by what he may realize tomorrow, force and fact becoming the norms of action. Surrealism, refusing any hereafter apart from this world and professing a doctrine of immanence, is nevertheless, inasmuch as it disqualifies the objective World, the messenger of some transcendence. This is why I have no trouble reconciling my admiration for André Breton and my admiration for Plato, Descartes, and Kant. For the rest, in what I say I commit only myself; obviously in no sense do I present myself as a spokesman for surrealism. It is from without that I have tried to define its philosophy. I do not claim to have retained all its richness nor to have explained it. Pondering what in surrealism might be conceptualized, I only hope I have not betrayed it.

Chapter One

The Surrealist Project

I. Hope and Love

"You are right, she tells me, the shadow here present is just now gone on horseback. The guides were formed from words of love, I think, but since the nostrils of fog and sachets of the blue have led you to this eternally banging door, come in and caress me all along these thought-strewn steps." [1]

If I place at the beginning of this book these old lines in which André Breton is dreaming of a maidservant inviting him to caresses, it is not only because when I was twenty the texts of *Poisson soluble* woke in me an emotion and a hope whose importance I recognized at once. *Poisson soluble* seems to me yet today, not certainly the strongest, but the most significant of surrealist works; it is, in any case, a key work. It is clear from the preceding text that quality and exactness of expression are not particularly studied. It may even be that Breton is not yet that perfect master of the language who, in 1949, could not admit that comparisons as mediocre as "taloned cats, hypocritical brides, enraged mammoths" had for an instant seduced Rimbaud. [2] From this point of view could we justify any more the "impeccable black coat" and the "beautiful white palpitating breasts" which he does not scruple to present us? [3] But, pre-

5

cisely, the search that sees the light first in *Poisson soluble* is not toward a discrete aesthetic quality. The several levels of activity are not distinguished; the text tends to bring forth an emotion and a hope addressed to man as a whole. And I am certain that Breton's emotion and his hope were, from the beginning, emotion before beauty and hope in beauty: the *Manifesto* even seems to seek in beauty alone a criterion for the value of an image.[4] Breton must travel a long way still before he realizes clearly what Beauty, considered in its essence, means to him, and before being able to write, in *Flagrant délit:* "Beauty is, in this area, the great refuge." [5] *Poisson soluble,* though it follows "five years of experimental activity," [6] is, as far as this realization goes, a point of departure, not a terminal. In no area is Breton then concerned with refuge, with analysis or even with reflection. To this extent all beauty that can be separated from life and objectified as spectacle appears literary, and literature is rejected. "Abstract your genius," says the *Manifesto,* "your talents and those of others. Admit that literature is one of the saddest paths leading anywhere." [7] Beauty—incapable of being objectified—can only be grasped in the heat of an excitement we would call existential if the word did not evoke now a completely different climate. We may call it "vital," if we remember that Breton's goal is to attain "real life" [8]— keeping always in mind that the word life is not used here as biologists use it but in the philosophic sense of existence. Living is not necessarily existing. Does not Breton write, at the end of the first *Manifesto:* "Living and ceasing to live are imaginary solutions. Existence is elsewhere." [9]

Prior to any critical development, to any reflection on itself, surrealism offers us a hope of existing and projects existence in something beyond natural life; an immanent beyond, however—not posterior to life—a beyond seeming to reveal itself to the one who will seize the World under the aspect of the marvelous. That this hope took, from the beginning, the face of sensually amorous joys, the text already cited will witness, as will most pages from *Poisson soluble,* where feminine images succeed each other without allowing us pause for breath. "Several maids came to meet me, dressed in tight-fitting suits of day-colored satin." [10] "She no longer turned toward me and without the abrupt glimmer of her calves which marked my path in flashes, I despaired of ever touching her. I was preparing nevertheless to join her again when she swung round and opening her coat revealed to me her nudity more enchanting than birds." [11] At a time when some condemn the surrealist emotion with a peevish assurance fostered by a disappointed boy scout's sensitiveness, it seems in place to insist on the admirable eroticism (a bit fetishist and obsessive, like anything that bespeaks passion) of most of Breton's automatic texts. Writing, "We reduce art to its simplest expression, which is love," [12] Breton remains faithful to Plato, who made no separation between the excitement before beauty and erotic excitement, and who always described the latter as an upheaval.[13] It is important then not to reduce the desire animating surrealism to a desire for sensual satisfactions. Quite the contrary, the amorous emotion appears in *Poisson soluble* as the unique goal of human search only because it contains all the obscurity, all the problems, all the ambiguity of man. No doubt the surrealists had not yet, in 1924, really analysed the notion of Beauty any more than that of love. But the women who haunt *Poisson soluble* are not the easy mistresses of libertine novels. They are harbingers of the new Eve, always placed beyond our desires.[14] They are the bond, and like a bridge, between waking and dream, and they seem to promise a reconciliation of the two. Breton takes care to set them in another element, for example "at the bottom of the water." "It is hard to imagine the number of women gliding in these depths, our changing guests. They, they also, are clothed in glass, naturally; some join to that monotonous accoutrement one or two gayer attributes—hats trimmed in wood shavings, veils of spider web, gloves and sunflower parasol." [15] In their company, Breton can maintain he has no heart for the earth.[16] He can even announce his absence from earth, and his return, "to all those women [who] will remain faithful" to him without "having known" him. "Comb your hair for him, comb it ceaselessly, he asks nothing else. He is not here, but he will return . . ." [17]

Thus, whatever enrichments and uncertainties the surrealist conception of love might come to know later, it is obvious that one of the first ferments of Breton's research was the desire to exist in love and to come, by love, to happiness; this is why the climate of *Poisson soluble* is all clarity and why it remains inexact to speak, as many have, of surrealist pessimism.[18] With the exception of text 9, and perhaps of text 12, everything in *Poisson soluble* indicates that the thirst for happiness colors all the spirit's motions and, in particular, precedes the attitudes of negation and revolt that are only its other side. Chronologically, no doubt, surrealism succeeded Dada negativity. But Breton was never at home in the Dada movement; he never saw in its revolt and its negation anything but the necessary means for the positive realization of man. This realization is his first goal. It attracts him and seems to give him a sign from the very sky: "See those marvelous horsemen. Far away, high up, from where return is uncertain, they throw their marvelous lasso made of a woman's two arms." [19] Breton does not go on to ask, as he will ask later, "What sort of hope is it you place in love?" [20] Love, emotion, hope, happiness—all these, for him, are one. And certainly such optimism is not common. Texts of automatic writing translating profoundly their author's personality, we cannot be surprised to find in the *Révolution surréaliste* texts of anguish, horror, and despair. "Die at last even to the sound of your strings the blood-flecked strings of your bones of your love filthy filthy filthy . . ."

Pierre Unik will write.[21] And Claude-André Puget, after evoking a love crucified in one ecstatic moment, ends his text by returning to a lover's deception which seems to me inseparable from a movement of critical reflection and some feeling of culpability: "Ha! this smoke, these ashes in my mouth . . . Obsidian! filthy succubus! Then it's you again!"[22] But these movements and feelings are rare with Breton; he is the one who gives surrealism its tone, and the marvelous, enraptured hope that engendered the images of *Poisson soluble* will be found again in *Nadja* and in *L'Amour fou*. We may consider then that, taken as a whole, the texts obtained from automatic writing are produced by a burst of hope in life. This hope makes aesthetic considerations and literary hierarchies appear paltry and beside the point. And certainly in the numberless pages written under Breton's impetus, bad taste is not absent. But Breton had said, "In the bad taste of my epoch I strive to go farther than any other."[23] They wrote at that time without fear, without reserve, and if ever the famous "poetry by everybody" was nearly realized, it was then. Many were convinced, not without naiveté, of the end of literature and of all aesthetically founded distinctions of value. At least, it was thought total man will take the place of literature and tables of value.

It would be of the highest interest to retrace the lifelines of those who then formed the surrealist group, those the *Manifesto* declares "have performed the absolute surrealist act."[24] One would discover in each of them, among actions apparently quite different, a strange identity of inspiration. During the period 1924 to 1926, Breton seemed like the poet of wonder, of confidence in man, of the universalization of happiness by wonderful love descending to earth. Eluard and Aragon —though not yet having cast, as they would later, in favor of the individual's submission to History and the State—bring to the surrealist ideal, on the contrary, modifications which, considered by their consequences, can only be revealed as its negation pure and simple. One is the distinction that, in the flyer for his book *Les Dessous d'une vie ou la Pyramide humaine,* Eluard establishes between the surrealist text, the dream and the poem—a distinction taken up by *La Révolution sur-réaliste,* the contents pages of which divided these three kinds of writing. Of poems, Eluard writes, "It is indispensable to know that they are the consequence of a sufficiently defined will, the echo of a formulated hope or despair." [25] Georges Hugnet finds this analysis "quite just"; [26] it is just, in fact, from the point of view of logic, of traditional aesthetics, and of everyday common sense, that is to say, from the point of view of everything surrealism had attempted to surpass. Certainly, no one before Breton had confounded a dream and a poem; so to distinguish them called for no great invention but a simple return to the general opinion. Eluard's affirmation formulated in 1926 could, in that way, have but one sense: it is necessary to give up the search—the only new and characteristic search in surrealism—for the unity of texts as distinct in appearance as the relating of a dream, a page of automatic writing, and a poem. And we see that one of the essential problems facing surrealism will be that of the status of beauty; Eluard's distinction is only a return to the idea of an aesthetic value separable from existence, an idea whose value we can certainly appreciate, but must recognize that it assumes a conception of beauty contemplated rather than possessed, beauty as spectacle and not as life, and hence the renunciation of happiness. Such a conception is simply the classic one. And the poems of Eluard very quickly regained a beauty of the classic type, certainly admirable all round, but capable of being recognized by readers completely alien to surrealism:

Your eyes are back from an arbitrary land
Where no one has ever known what a glance is
Or known the beauty of eyes, beauty of stones . . .

The blinding sun serves you as mirror
And if it seems to obey the evening powers
It is because your head is closed, O broken statue . . .[27]

The evening trailed white weapons over our heads
Courage consumed the women among us . . .[28]

Remembrances of green timber, fog into which I plunge,
I have closed my eyes on myself, I am yours . . .[29]

and

> *As the day is upheld by innocence*
> *The whole world hangs from your pure eyes . . .*[30]

lines I have always found identical to those pronounced
by Racine's dying Phædra:

> *And death, cutting off the light from my eyes,*
> *Gives day back all the purity they stained.*[31]

The quarrel between Aragon and Breton seems still
more grave. "We have no talent," [32] Breton declares, and
is pleased to think of himself as a recording apparatus or
a mirror. "What I have done, what I have not done, I
give to you." [33] The mere idea that talent might be uni-
versalized sends Aragon on the contrary, by all indica-
tions, into the greatest fury: "Under pretext that this is
all surrealism," he writes, "the next cur who happens
along thinks himself authorized to equate his little slob-
berings with true poetry, a marvelous comfort for vanity
and stupidity." [34] And, by an inevitable consequence,
hope and happiness do not get from Aragon any great
welcome. "There is no hope," "there is nothing to wait
for," "there is no paradise of any kind," [35] and, "you
really think happiness an aim for your life? You think it
exists?" [36]

Here someone may point out that with Breton himself
the search for happiness sometimes seems to be condemned. "I will sacrifice nothing for happiness: prag-

matism is outside my scope," he says in *Les Pas perdus*.[37]
And, in the *Manifesto:* "To reduce the imagination to
slavery, even though there would be in this what is vulgarly called happiness, is to pull back from all we find in
the depths of ourselves of supreme justice." [38] But who
cannot see that "what is vulgarly called happiness" is not
happiness as Breton understands it, happiness that cannot survive the sacrifice of love. What Breton condemns
is, as he says, pragmatism, the calculated and calculating
search for a limited and prudent happiness, demanding
the renunciation of the dream and of the essential exigencies of desire. It is by worry for this happiness that the
majority of men consent precisely to separate beauty from
their lives, to regard it as abstract and formal, to hang it on
the wall to contemplate on Sunday, while living during
the week the life of everybody or, as Breton puts it, "the
life of dogs." [39] But the lightning bolts that incessantly
flash across *Poisson soluble* are exact images of happiness,
rips through which we can see it, with the rapture and the
staggering excitement it produces. "Daughters of the
blue sepulcher, holidays, forms rung from the angelus of
my eyes and from my head when I awaken, customs of
flame-shaped provinces, you bring me the sun of white
woodwork, mechanical sawmills, and wine. This is my
pale angel, my hands so reassured. Seagulls from paradise lost!" [40] Without wishing to propose a religious interpretation of surrealism, we may note that the word
"paradise" is pronounced here, that we meet the term
"salvation" on the third page of the *Manifesto*, that it is
further stated that poetry "bears in itself the perfect compensation for the miseries that we endure," and that he
hopes it will "break solely the bread of heaven for the
earth." [41] We do not hesitate to add that *Poisson soluble*
seems to us to illustrate better than any other text, not
Gide's affirmation, "Surely all nature teaches that man is
made for happiness," [42] but this of Bossuet, at the beginning of his *Méditations sur l'Evangile:* "The whole aim
of man is to be happy." [43] For "nature" teaches nothing

to an imagination whose whole aspiration is to surpass nature. But happiness is inseparable from the very principle of that imagination, a principle that Breton never better defined than in writing, "Liberty, color of man." [44]

Nevertheless, it is in this world and this world only that Breton wishes to find happiness, and to find it by love. Thus, he condemns the religious attitude, retaining only its human aspiration. His paradise regained must be that of everyday life, everyday life transfigured. In *Poisson soluble* it is the life of Paris, and of a Paris ceaselessly transformed into the most marvelous, the most luminous abode of love. "The *place du Porte Manteau,* all windows open this morning, is furrowed by taxis with green flags and by private vehicles. Beautiful inscriptions in silver letters spread to all stories the names of bankers, of famous racers." [45] "The woman with ermine breasts was posted at the entry to the *passage Jouffroy,* illuminated by songs. She needed no great prompting to follow me." [46] "Having rented a most luxuriously furnished apartment, every evening we presented marvelous entertainments. The entry of the *Porte Albinos* in a gown with an immense train was always a sensation." [47] "The auto now rambled about, its hands gloved in rubber, over the furnishings of the Paris-room." [48] "The landscape of Paris, nightingale of the world, varied from moment to moment and amid the tapers of her coiffeurs shot forth her pretty spring trees." [49] "One of the magnetic poles of my route should be, I had long known, the luminous sign for 'Longines' at the angle of the *Rue de la Paix* and the *Place de l'Opera.*" [50] The romantics, captives of the nostalgia for religion, dreamed of departure, of local color and historic color, of exoticism; they revealed in this the profound link that unites, in man, the desire for another world and the desire for a world situated elsewhere in space and time. For the surrealists, real life is here. "I always forbade myself to think of the future," says Breton; [51] Paris therefore replaces Venice and the forests of America, the present reveals to man the sum of his

powers. So Aragon could ridicule the thirst for departure, for adventure, for escape,[52] and Breton could write,
"I hold Paris like—to tell your future—your open
hand." [53] We know how far Breton will extend this
Parisian fairyland: all *Nadja's* readers remember the
evocation of the "statue of Etienne Dolet, *place Mau-*
bert" [54] or "the luminous poster for Mazda on the grand
boulevards." [55] With regard to the *Pont Neuf, La Clé des*
champs distinguishes more rigorously than any other text
what, in Breton's excitement, results from the form of the
landscape, from "what has taken place here or there,"
from analogy, from correspondences, from magic causal-
ities; [56] we gather that one of the reasons that led Breton
to reduce adventure and everyday life to one and the
same thing was a perception of the urban setting itself
as feminine: "If for a second you attribute to the Seine
the gesture of letting the arm she held bent against her
forehead glide along her thigh like a woman. . . ." [57] And
such is doubtless the deepest source of the feeling, constant with Breton, that the street should be the place of
his essential encounters. "The street, which I believed
could offer my life its surprising detours, the street with
its uneasinesses and its glances, was my true element:
there as nowhere else I caught the breath of the possible," [58] Breton writes in 1924. And in 1952, reminiscing
to André Parinaud of his "solicitation" at seventeen, he
speaks of the "solemn afterthought that it is there, in the
streets' chances, that whatever really relates [to him] is
called into play," whatever concerns him in particular,
whatever is deeply linked to his fate.[59]

An analogous inspiration illuminates some of the pages
of Aragon's *Le Paysan de Paris*. But there it sometimes
seems borrowed, and numerous texts consecrated to
Paris drift toward a sensuality completely physical,
sometimes even gastronomical, reminiscent more of Léon
Daudet in his *Paris vécu*.[60] Aragon speaks with unexcep-
tionable authenticity when he speaks of women and of
voluptuousness: the fetish of blondness,[61] the vertigo of

pleasure,[62] excitement before prostitution,[63] inspire admirable pages. And I think the lover's excitement in Aragon, shot through with libertinism and subject to the
baffling vertigo of the present, has played—alongside
that of Breton and that of Eluard—a determining role in
the elaboration of surrealist eroticism. But in Aragon and
Eluard, Paris and Nature give place entirely to woman
proper. In Breton they are themselves permeated by
femininity, thus permitting hope to become expectation
and expectation to take on a value and an ontological
sense. You may be sure, Breton will write in *Nadja,* "not
more than three days will pass without seeing me come
and go, late in the afternoon, through the *boulevard
Bonne-Nouvelle,* between the printing office of the *Matin*
and the *boulevard de Strasbourg.* I do not know why it
is my steps carry me there, that nearly always I find myself
going without definite aim, with nothing decisive except that obscure premise, namely that it will happen
there(?)" [64] Penetrated by uneasiness as this text seems
in some ways to be, it is difficult not to recognize the echo
of a positive hope, and of the presentiment that happiness may be discovered in everyday life. Now the problem of finding human happiness in this life, and by the
sole modification of our attitude toward life, is a problem
the whole Christian era has neglected, Christianity judging happiness possible only in the supernatural order.
To find the search for happiness and the idea of the
World's sufficiency united, we must go back to pagan
antiquity. And even the ancient solution, as seen in
Stoicism, was always renunciation. Here, on the contrary,
hope is possessive, sacrifices no desire, and seems set to
wait for some mysterious accord between our demands
and the course of things. This hope exists before any
conscious project, before any defined method; this is why
we have looked for the first image of it in the texts of
Poisson soluble. Aragon declares that "the documentary
value" of a surrealist text "is that of a photograph." [65] In
contemplating *Poisson soluble* as a photograph, we shall

discover Breton prey to an expectation which, at its origin, is justified only by an irreducible but irrational certitude: that in all things a sign of love may be found.

II. Existence and Literature

Surrealism is life. What matters to it is not making literary works, but exteriorizing human forces, loving, hoping, and discovering. "From literature and—if we could say so—from the sheet of paper," Georges Hugnet writes, "poetry has thereby slipped to the center of life. It is no longer an art, a spiritual state, but life, spirit." [66] Here Jean Paulhan accuses surrealism, and with it realism, of bad faith. He wants neither "human document" nor "superhuman document." "I am astonished," he writes, "to see you begin with a lie. For you still *write*, though you are against writing and are aware of it." [67] We must grant Paulhan that its relation with aesthetics and with literature is the most serious problem the surrealist attitude will raise. But the simple fact that the surrealists have written is not enough to pose this problem. A diplomatic note, an ultimatum, a medical prescription, a law book, an insulting letter are all writings. Who would claim from this that they are literary works? For that, it would be necessary that the author, separating himself a moment from his essential aim, thought of language as such—let us not even say from the point of view of form or of rhetoric, but in order to ask if it is adapted to its end. The attitude of one who speaks or writes in order to inform, to intimidate, to produce passion, to heal, to wound, to tell of an experience, without once considering by itself the language serving as means, is certainly not literary. And we must take care not to ascribe to the author of a text the aesthetic vision of the reader. The reader approaches the text, finding it already written, and thus a token from the past. Seizing the past is always, to some extent, aesthetic; history and time have been realized for us and without us, the separation from the living that is the first condition of artistic vision. But the work which for us is art was art for its author only if, in regard to it, he took that step back which makes spectacle possible, the way the painter stops painting to look at what he has painted. The artisans of the *Pont du Gard* did not see in it a Roman monument embellishing the landscape; they constructed an aqueduct. The inspiration of many surrealist texts, likewise, may be found only when we cease coming to these texts with an aesthetic point of view, or in the spirit of an amateur of ruins.

So the numerous pages in surrealist works that relate experiments pose above all a problem of truth and of sense. Whether the pages are beautiful may be questioned, but it is certainly not the question. The question, as in a treatise on physics, is to know if the experience related is transcribed objectively, to discover its significance and its range. Take the narrative that closes *L'Amour fou.*[68] On July 20, 1936, about three in the afternoon, Breton and his wife get off a bus "in the proximity of a narrow beach near Lorient: the *Fort Bloqué.*" They begin walking on the sand, but feel an anxiety mixed with despondency and this separates them. Breton throws stones at the sea birds, which irritate him. He notices a house that appears lugubrious to him, an enclosure that seems to him bounded by wire fencing. Passing a stream he suffers "panic desire to go back the way he came." Then, once past a small fort, everything settles: "...we had no trouble agreeing," Breton writes, "that the torment we had just endured was founded on nothing that, in reality, endangered our love." Returning to Lorient, Breton learns from relatives that the stream crossed is the Loch and the house they passed by the "Loch villa," where Michel Henriot killed his young wife with a hunting rifle. In the outbuildings of the house, Henriot had indulged in raising silver foxes. Before the murder, Michel Henriot and his wife had been emotionally apart, as were for an instant Breton and her he nevertheless loved. "Michel Henriot was in the habit of shooting sea birds for pleasure," and Breton put "these same birds to flight with stones." On the eve of the trip, a friend had loaned Breton's wife two books: Mary Webb's *Gone to Earth* [69] and *Lady into Fox* by David Garnett; these two volumes, and only the two, had been brought to Brittany. Finally, Breton, returning to the site, saw that "the enclosure that had constituted the park with the foxes was closed in," not—as he had believed he saw—"by wire fencing, but ... by a concrete wall," completely cutting off from the outside any view of "the cages of wire fencing" which as a matter of fact—but inside—adjoined this wall. "It was as if on July 20, this wall appeared" "transparent" for Breton. Add to this that the little fort beyond which the uneasiness cleared was for a time the dwelling of Michel Henriot and his wife; thus, the very limits of the antecedent tragedy were where Breton and his wife seemed victims of "deleterious emanations, emanations attacking the very principle of the moral life." And Breton can think that "the mirror of love between two beings" is subject to "confusion from the fact of circumstances totally foreign to that love, and to recovering in an instant at the expiration of these circumstances." Who will not agree that the literary problems posed by the manner in which a text is written are here void of interest? An awkward, clumsy narrative telling us the same thing would have the same value. What matters is the content, not the form of the testimony. Are Breton's recollections exact?—complete? What are the probabilities for pure coincidence in this affair? May we conclude, from the facts stated, that certain places possess a magic nimbus capable of dissolving our liberty, delivering us to tragic but impersonal structures, shaping our gestures, modifying our thoughts and sentiments, able to change our very love into an anxiety of separation? These are the questions, and the only questions, this adventure raises.

And how many other narratives in surrealist works

likewise wrench us away from literature, bringing to birth in us an interrogation that we may call scientific or philosophic but which is certainly not aesthetic! Here we must recall that the surrealists wanted first of all to explore the unconscious, madness, hallucinatory states, the "phrases more or less partial that in full solitude, at the approach of sleep, become perceptible to the spirit," [70] and the images which accompany these phrases (such as, for Breton, "the faint visual representation of a man walking and truncated by a window perpendicular to the axis of his body").[71] To discover such images, to test their force, the surrealists rendered themselves passive, appealed to hypnotic sleep: this is the "wave of dreams," [72] the "entrance of the mediums," [73] the exploration of all the states we might call "second states." René Crevel, in 1922, having entertained his friends "with the start of a spiritualistic initiation for which he was obliged to a lady D...," they soon organize seances in common. Crevel goes into a sleep, speaks with a "declamatory diction, interrupted by sighs, sometimes breaking into song," and on waking "retains no memory of his narrative." [74] Then it is Desnos' turn, who—in sleep—writes and sketches in reply to questions:

Q—What do you know of Péret?
R—He will die in coach full of people.
Q—Will he be assassinated?
R—Yes.
Q—By whom?
R—(He draws a train, a man falling from the door.) By an animal.
Q—By what animal?
R—A blue ribbon my sweet tramp.[75]

In the course of one of these seances, Benjamin Péret "rises precipitately without being asked, throws himself stomach down on the table and simulates swimming." [76] No doubt we may ask here if some dissimulation may not have entered into the figures. For my part I remain skeptical about the reality of the hypnotic sleeps. However that may be, the rapidity of delivery would seem to exclude any preconsidered fabrication. This is why gestures and discourse translate the deeper personality of each, the anxiety that already rules Crevel, the "romantic taste for shipwreck" [77] of Desnos. It is also why such "sleep" provokes profound troubles in those who enter it, liberating "an impulsive activity from which one should fear the worst." [78] Crevel and several others eventually try to hang themselves; Desnos, pursuing Eluard with a knife, has to be overpowered. So Breton puts an end to these experiments. But for all that, the spirit that inspired them is not abandoned. The activity of the "Bureau of Surrealist Research," opened at 15 rue de Grenelle, directed by Francis Gérard and then Antonin Artaud, carries it forward.

Nadeau has good reason, then, to say: "The surrealists are harnessed to a research in the same manner as the scholar who moves into unknown territory, supported only by a hypothesis that he believes correct but that it is important to verify." [79] At best the hypothesis that supports the surrealists cannot be clearly formulated, and their experiments resemble rather what Claude Bernard calls "experiments in order to see"; [80] such is the case of the trip, undertaken at random and in hope of no particular adventure, by Breton, Aragon, Morise and Vitrac, starting from Blois, a "town drawn by lot from the map." [81] But directed by precise hypotheses or not, surrealist activity escapes from rhetoric; it endeavors to extend human experience, to interpret it outside the limits and framework of a narrow rationalism, to take—in a word—the measure of man. And it has recourse, for this, to many other means than those of language: studying the automatic message,[82] Breton invokes the visual images of Herschel, the vision of Watt, the seer's crystal ball, the forms and scenes that Leonardo da Vinci recommended his students to search for on old walls, the specimens of ornamented script that Marcel Til com-

municated to Flournoy, the architecture of the mailman
Cheval, the etching of Victorien Sardou ("The House of
Mozart on the Planet Jupiter"), the Medianimic drawings,[83] the transformation in Saint Teresa's eyes of her
wooden cross into a crucifix of precious stones—none of
these messages is verbal or in the province of literature.
Surrealism is the search for a path of knowledge and salvation, it is attention to everything that lifts man above
himself or seems at least to draw him out of himself. It
wishes to escape "from the constraints weighing on su-
pervised thought," [84] from the tyranny of the laws of the
sensible world, from the critical spirit, from the taboos
of the current morality, from everything that corrects
and dams up, and to recover, once again, the total liberty
of man. The marvelous love, the hope of existence, the
excitement of streets, which give surrealism its color,
are not without relation to the epoch of the hypnotic
sleeps (which *Poisson soluble* followed). In every case
there is manifested a right-of-way to the world of the
dream, the place where those promises may be kept that
seem pledged to us in everyday reality by love and
beauty. In the most revelatory manner, Breton, insinuat-
ing that perceiving nothing in the fortune-teller's crystal
ball may be from some "bad will," [85] adds: "I think it
necessary never to have been alone, never to have had
time to give way to this marvel of hope which makes
the real presence of the loved being surge from total
absence, not—at least theoretically—to caress with the
eyes this object, among all objects anonymous and unreasonable, this ball, empty in broad sunlight, that in the
shadow contains all." [86] We cannot speak here of "synthesis" between the real world and the world of dreams,
nor of their unity, but as Breton will say, of "means to
pass at will" and "as if it were enough to press a but-
ton" [87] from one to the other. The prestige of Desnos,
which *Nadja* will mention,[88] comes from the facility with
which he manages this passage, clearing the bridge. And
surrealist liberty will always consist in this same facility:

the surrealist object, deflected from its utilitarian sense, the surrealist games, where responses at random are mated with precise questions, have no other aim than to sensitize the spirit to a similar appeal, to persuade it that it wrongly neglects its power of returning whenever it likes to the land where, in the admirable line of Baudelaire, everything would speak to him in "in his sweet native tongue." [89]

But for all that we have not escaped from the problem of language as Paulhan has posed it. Removed from language, the surrealist experience could have become in effect mystical, spiritualist, occultist. From the beginning Breton underlines his distrust in regard to spiritualism, from which he consents only to borrow methods. He refuses to admit "the exogeneity of the dictating principle, in other words the existence of spirits." [90] Far from seeing in poetry the sign of the beyond, Aragon reduces the beyond to poetry.[91] And in 1947 Breton again demonstrates great prudence in the problem of the relations between surrealism and magic. "We intend," he writes, "to leave to specialists of the occult the responsibility for deciding, all pieces in hand, if a certain number of poetic works ... have been conceived in close liaison with what its adepts take for the first religious, moral, and political doctrine of humanity, or if they derive more or less consciously from it, or if they tend—completely intuitively—to recreate it by other ways." [92] And he is content to say that "everything happens today as if such relatively recent poetic and plastic works held a power over the spirit exceeding in every sense that of works of art ... as if those works were marked with the seal of revelation." [93] Let us add to this that Breton has never entered into the hypnotic sleep,[94] and that his taste for self control and lucidity turned the rest of the group from this practice. On the other hand, he prefers the verbal message to any other. "I hold," he writes, "and this is essential, that verbal inspirations are infinitely richer in visual sense, infinitely stronger to the

eye, than visual images proper." [95] Automatic writing
thus replaces more and more, in surrealism, every other
means of investigation (as in the elaboration of Freud's
method free association takes the place of hypnosis).
From there on, how avoid keeping "only fragments of
the message, considered as choicest"? [96] In 1933, however, Breton is indignant at this. The phrase cited at
the opening of his study of the automatic Message:
"Oh no, no, I bet Bordeaux Saint Augustine ... There's
a notebook in that" [97] is certainly chosen for its lack of
literary value. Careful to proclaim "the complete equality
of all normal human beings before the subliminal message," [98] Breton condemns "the execrable poetic rivalry"
and affirms that the aesthetic attitude, "instinctive
on the part of men exercised in appreciating poetic
value, has had the unfortunate consequence of giving
the recording subject an immediate grasp on each part
of the recorded message." [99] Yet in 1952 Breton decided
"that is not as important as it might seem." [100] In fact,
since 1933 he was aware, not perhaps without some
contradiction to the idea of equality before the message,
that hypnosis liberates talents and promotes the rise of
faculties not necessarily the same in everybody. [101] Might
one not fear, consequently, that as far as experimental
research is concerned surrealism has undergone a sort
of degradation, going from the message to automatic
writing and from automatic writing to the poem?

No doubt those who would like to connect surrealism
with occultism proper would say yes. I think on the contrary that the apparent decline of the surrealist experience
and its reduction to language were not a degradation
but a return to its essence, which is poetry. Poetry is in
effect the bridge which unites the world of everyday
reality with that of the marvelous dream, and this bridge
remains the only bridge for whoever would retain lucidity, not interpreting signs of the transcendent in the
language of a hypothetical, religious, or magical dogmatism. I do not presume to decide the future of surrealism

or to foresee what Breton will one day think or say. But it is possible to affirm that the sources of surrealism are not to be found in esoterism. The young men at the time of the hypnotic sleeps must have been only slightly versed in such matters and we have seen Crevel make much of a recent and superficial spiritualist initiation. On the other hand, at the very moment in his life when he is declaring "the demon that possesses me is not the literary demon," [102] Breton, a stranger and as if absent in university classrooms (he was then a medical student), cares only to watch and to approach poets. All that finds grace in his eyes is "what poetry and art have been able to produce of the most rare." [103] Above all, he admires "bearing," "quality," "nobility of expression." [104] He himself writes Mallarméan poems:

Of green gold the ripe grapes and my futile wishes
Gorging with so sweet a brightness I am stunned
With the artless delight of encompassing your hair,
Most beautiful, to envy only the monotonous azure . . .[105]

He pays a visit to Vielé-Griffin, to Valéry. So he will write to his daughter at the end of *L'Amour fou:* "You issued from the single reflection of what for me was rather late, the fulfillment of poetry, to which I dedicated myself in my youth, poetry which I have continued to serve, despising all else." [106] And Aragon, who could not always acknowledge the same fidelity to poetry, declares in his *Traité du style,* "Yes, I read. I am ridiculous that way. I love beautiful poems, staggering lines, and the whole beyond of those lines. I am sensitive like no one else to these poor marvelous words left in our night by some men I have not known. I love poetry." [107] The passage to poetry, then, was not a fall for the surrealists, nor a step ahead; it was a return, and a return to what they had never left.

But it is important not to confound poetry and literature. Literature is rejected by the surrealists in the name of poetry. Poetry is the domain of the marvelous, and "the marvelous is always beautiful, any marvelous is beautiful, nothing but the marvelous is beautiful." [108] Poetry does not interest us the way a narrative does; it transforms us by the emotion it brings to birth. Poetry is the field of our liberty and permits us to give to all things the form of our desires. The attempt at collecting the profound forces of our spirit "may be regarded as well the province of poets as of scholars." [109] On the other hand, Breton formally condemns the novel.[110] He condemns it because it is anecdote, because it is necessarily under the sway of logic, because its object remains outside us, because in it every human character is necessarily coherent and determined, because construction keeps an upper hand over direct emotion. "I wish," Breton says, "those who no longer feel would be silent." [111] If then Breton, rejecting literature, is confident in poetry, it is that poetry appears to him ontological, vital; it seems to him to possess the keys of liberty, to contain the message of human happiness, and that in the measure of its being the original language, the only true language, expressing being and creating its object. The poet is neither æsthete nor entertainer. He is the one who promises, reveals, and realizes. His promise, the promise of "real life," Breton perceived first, in the midst of overwhelming emotions, in the "But how salubrious the wind!" of Rimbaud, the "Alors, comme la nuit vieillissait" of Mallarmé after Poe, above all perhaps in that advice from a mother to her daughter in a tale by Louÿs: "Beware ... young men who pass along the roads with the evening wind and winged dust." [112] For the rest, he avows his "profound insensibility before natural spectacles and works of art which do not, straightway, procure a physical disturbance characterized by a gust of wind at the temples capable of bringing a true thrill," and envisages beauty as "concerned with emotional aims exclusively." [113] Between poetic emotion and erotic pleasure he finds only "a difference in degree." [114] Then, asking what poetry really delivers and reveals, he tries to extend its limits; it is there he recovers a moral preoccupation with universality. Aesthetics, already condemned as not vital and the source of the separation of the work from life, is now rejected as the fundament of the differences of value preventing men from all aspiring to poetry. And Breton, like all those who dream of universalizing a pleasure or a knowledge, enunciates a "method": automatic writing.[115] It is a matter of writing without preconceived subject and without logical, aesthetic or moral control, exteriorizing everything in us that tends to become language and normally finds itself impeded by our conscious surveillance. For everything in us is discourse or tendency toward discourse, but our consciousness reduces our discourse to what it inspires and controls, making our life, our anxieties, our gestures a language uncomprehended and alone, despairing so far that it no longer recognizes itself as language. By automatic writing Breton aspires to liberate and manifest this essential discourse which man is. This method inclines surrealism toward science, in which only, in effect, can one really speak of method, of universality, and of revelation of a logos up to that point hidden. And yielding, from this fact, to the necessary postulates of every science, Breton makes his goal objective and speaks of the "real function" of thought, which automatic writing would allow to be brought to light. The *Manifesto* defines surrealism thus: "Pure psychic automatism by which we propose to express, whether verbally or by writing or by any other manner, the real function of thought ... surrealism rests on the belief in the higher reality of certain forms of association neglected heretofore." [116]

But why is the unconscious functioning of thought called more real than its rational functioning? How do "certain forms of association" possess a "higher reality" than logical progression or attention? One cannot, it seems, furnish quite satisfactory answers to these questions, and while Breton's vocabulary attempts to be scientific

it is probably inadequate. Monnerot, rightly astonished
by the expression "real function," suggests substituting
for the term "reality" the term "value." Breton refers, he
writes, "to a hierarchy of values set up against the
abandoning of certain human properties that are no
longer quite respectable . . ." And he adds: "'It is only too
certain that an interior discourse or a flux of images
born without warning in us, in spite of us, without us,
could not without paralyzing confusion be called thought
or be recognized as higher in principle than everything
produced in other ways . . . If the obscure does not enclose what is most precious, if the oppressed is not worth
more than what oppresses it, what remains of the obscure
and the oppressed, of their pretension to supreme domin-
ion over our souls? . . ." [117] Without necessarily accepting
the expression "real function of thought" (born no doubt
under the influence of a conception of psychoanalysis
according the unconscious an ontological "reality" that
clear consciousness would possess only to a lesser degree), I think we might reply to Monnerot's profound
question by speaking, not of illusory degrees of reality
for thought, but of the reality of the worlds to which
thought refers. Without a doubt, in fact, automatic
thought is called more real because it partakes of poetry,
which in turn reveals the world of surreality, the world
that Breton in the *Manifesto* grants "absolute reality"—
and legitimately this time to the extent that this world
appears to him to make good the synthesis of visible
world and imaginary world.[118] Still, to accept such an
interpretation we must renounce seeing in poetry a
"magic without hope." "The very essence of magic,"
says Monnerot, "is only nocturnal belief in the efficacy
of desire and of sentiment . . . But when poetry is no
longer anything but poetry . . . the operation is not accompanied by the hope of results, by which magic resembles science. Poetry is magic for the sake of magic,
magic without hope . . . the incantation ceases to seek
its aim outside itself, the appeal does not expect fulfill-

ment, poetry is prayer in a void." [119] In these remarkable formulas, Monnerot defines a poetry resolutely limited to the field of the imaginary and fully aware of this. And one could claim that all poetry should be so. But surrealist poetry was assuredly not so, at least in its initial project. It was not content to "overdetermine" the phenomenon "by a poetic sense" capable of "seeing it completely otherwise," superimposing itself on the useful; it did not search for "substitute satisfactions." [120] Issued from the original language, by which—before all reflection—the essential exigency of man expresses itself, it wanted to transform life and even, as we shall see, the World (we know what attraction the Revolution held for surrealism). We are not saying that such a project was coherent, or practicable; we do say that it was the fundamental project of surrealism, a project in which poetry, existence, love, and hope were not distinguished.

Despite a hesitant vocabulary in which the word "art" sometimes means what Breton condemns and sometimes what he praises, the surrealist position is quite clear. What Breton does not want, what he rejects under the name of literature, is a beauty separated from life, from love, from human hope, the formal beauty that expresses without creating, relates without transforming. In his letter to Rolland de Renéville, Breton is most indignant at being accused of coming round to "poetry-as-means-of-expression." [121] Poetry never ceased for Breton to be life, to assume the face of the world that one must realize, and of the liberty of man who will realize this world. One of the first poems of Breton, written in 1913 and dedicated to Valéry, joins with the eroticism of the marvelous:

> *But enraptured by her in disrobed whiteness*
> *That realities have not yet enslaved . . .*

the tragic interrogation:

> *In whom do you hope? From where your faith in life?* [122]

Posing a similar question to Breton in 1924, we believe we should hear him reply: in poetry itself.

III. Experience and System

All members of the surrealist group admitted the opposition between poetry as "means of expression" and poetry as "activity of the spirit." But doubtless it did not have the same sense for each. The article of Tristan Tzara, "Essay on the Situation of Poetry," [123] entirely based on this opposition, seems in spite of several of his formulas to express an attitude quite different from Breton's. As a matter of fact, Tzara does not conceal that he is a stranger to the emotion-revelation, that he detests the marvelous; his concern seems to be to reconcile the negative spirit of Dada—which he has obviously not renounced—and a supposed dialectical materialism hastily drawn from Engels. We look in vain here for the field of delight or even for poetic significance. The only citations in the article are: "hop! hop! hop!" (Burger) and

Ah!

Eh! Hé!

Hi! hi! hi!

Oh!

Hu! hu! hu! hu! hu!

(Charles Lassailly)

Here we are far from the wind of Rimbaud or the aging night of Mallarmé! Tzara, indeed, remains the one who in 1921, in *Littérature,* gave the rating of minus 25 (the lowest possible) to Baudelaire, to Nerval, to Poe, and minus 1 to Rimbaud.[124] I believe such collaborators have helped mask to many the positive human value surrealism has always granted to true poetry. And one might claim that in recognizing this value surrealism approaches the tradition of literature. This is true, however, only to the extent that the great writers have never been, as some would like to believe, partisans of the indefensible doctrine of art for art's sake. If Breton, desirous of changing life, comes back to them, it is not because he is diluting his own project; it is because they were concerned with lifting man up, with proposing an ideal of dignity and grandeur in which the exigencies of man would no longer be scorned.

We know that Breton always maintained, in his critical judgments, the primacy of the moral point of view. An ethical demand and a general conception of existence and of the human condition dominate him; in their name he exalts or condemns literary productions, paintings, or films, refusing in each case to be limited to examining their formal qualities. But what writer worthy the name ever refused this criterion? If it has been possible to oppose art and morality, it is in confounding morality with the prejudiced, hypocritical imbeciles who attacked *Tartuffe*, the judges who condemned Baudelaire. Is it not clear, on the contrary, that in the work of Molière and Baudelaire we find not only aesthetic value but authentic morality? True beauty is always moral and shows us what man must be. In applauding the lines of *Tartuffe* we reprove hypocrisy, and the emotion that Don Juan's boldness inspires makes us consent to a nature free of prejudices and even generous. Corneille's sublime heroism is indissolubly aesthetic and moral, and Bénichou has well shown that the literature of the seventeenth century expresses a long debate over the relation of man and values,[125] the nobility of Corneille's hero being soon contested by the naturalism of Molière, by the pessimism of La Rochefoucauld, by the rigor of the Jansenists discovering self-love as the principle of all the virtues. Literature has never been the work of pure aesthetes concerned only with technical or formal problems, nor, it goes without saying, of partisans of a moralizing art meant to propagate the orders of patronage or political lines. All beauty speaks to us of man, tells us what man must be. On this point Breton is no innovator.

Neither does Breton renounce the larger part of the literary tradition. Trying, in the *Manifesto,* to find what writers before him were surrealist, he mentions with some reserve Dante and Shakespeare, and then finds some surrealism in Young, Swift, Sade, Chateaubriand, Constant, Hugo, Desbordes-Valmore, Bertrand, Rabbe, Poe, Baudelaire, Rimbaud, Mallarmé, Jarry, Nouveau, Saint-Pol-Roux, Fargue, Vaché, Reverdy, St.-John Perse, and Roussel.[126] Lautréamont, later to become the undisputed master, is only mentioned, and his case is called *"passionnant."* [127] The German romantics, the initiated, and the illuminati are not mentioned; no allusion is made to Novalis, Hölderlin, Nerval, or William Blake. Nothing shows better how Breton, who would eventually recognize them as his ancestors, did not find his inspiration in them; his project is personal, autonomous, he first searches among authors he knows—particularly French authors—for the presentiment. And what determines his choice is less the form or the style adopted by the writer than the conception of man that seems to prescribe his work; no doubt this is why Marceline Desbordes-Valmore, entirely abandoned to love, can be side by side with Roussel, Rimbaud, and Reverdy, and why Sade— who will never be renounced—is called "surrealist in sadism," that is, in the very essence of his attitude and of his emotion. Breton's project here grows more clear and precise. What beauty promises is the reconciliation of man with himself; the new age which beauty announces is the age in which reason will no longer be contrary to the totality of desire. In 1933 Breton will be able to place himself in the path opened by Lautréamont and Rimbaud, a path which (as opposed to spiritualism, which wishes to "dissociate the psychological personality of the medium") "proposes nothing less than unifying this personality." [128] During the time of the hypnotic slumbers, it was necessary to put up a bridge between the real world and that of the imaginary. Now it is necessary to confound them and thus discover the basic unity of man, who is their common source and the native ground of their opposition.

The nature of such an ambition explains the rupture of Breton with the classical tradition (from which we believe he recovers, in the most general sense, the moral project). What he refuses in this tradition is the idea of separation, of distinctness, and thus of renunciation, that dominates it. And again, aesthetic divergences are simply the consequence of moral divergences. Classicism opposed, in the work of art, form and content: Racine or La Fontaine did not hesitate to take over old themes to treat in new forms. The surrealist conception of a beauty overwhelming and vital destroys any such analysis. In fact, the surrealist idea of the passivity of dictation in automatic writing and the valorization of all phrases received thereby are the negation of the separation between inspiration, which furnishes at most a material for the work, and the methodical and selective toil which according to Boileau must follow it. But the classical distinction of form and content, of inspiration and creation, was merely the consequence of belief in a deeper separation, moral this time, which divides man against himself. The classical tradition separates reason—all that is truly human and raises us above the beasts—and, on the other side, instincts and sentiments common to man and beast and linked to the body. Thus, it is important to submit the lower parts of our being to reason. This is the conception that Breton refuses above all, and this refusal conditions all the others. To any interior separation of man, Breton, in the name of his hope in love and happiness, opposes the unity of spirit and desire. It is not hard to see that such a synthesis must lead to the collapse of the separation of man and World, that separation being the work of scientific reason, undertaking the objective determination of the real world by the rejection of any affective or imaginative construction.

In this sense the Cartesian conception is reversed. Certainly, the experience of dissatisfaction is common to Breton and Descartes, and when Carrouges, commenting on Breton, notes that if "man can be conscious of the base and mediocre character of his life, it is because he feels in the depth of his being the presence of infinite virtualities unalterably inscribed on the human spirit, even if he too often forgets them," [129] he is—perhaps without knowing it—strictly faithful to Descartes. But Descartes first meditated on the rigorous constraints of a rational and technological science, on the hardness of the world of the object. He thus connects the infinite of our virtualities with the infinite of the divine actuality, an infinite superior to the World we live in, an infinite about which our consciousness signifies only the reality and inaccessibility. It is then in the God of Descartes that we must search for the presentiment of the unified being Breton dreams of; this God is not subject to logical verities or rational constructions: he has freely created them. But the Cartesian man remains in the world and can master it only by submitting to its laws, accepting first of all the constraints of reason. For Breton, on the contrary, it is a question of discovering the infinite in our powers themselves, of actualizing directly and according to the paths of desire the totality of these powers, considered as capable of staggering the intimate order of the real, a real to which they feel some secret affinity. If man must become the master of Nature, it is in a new sense; here we are closer to a magical than to a scientific hope. There is no more question of reconstructing the World technologically by submitting to objective laws, remaking things according to properly mechanical processes differing from those by which Nature made them; we aspire to an upheaval, which as it transformed the World would at the same time change life. Hope in such an upheaval presupposes the kinship of the powers which construct the Universe and the priniciples that direct our thoughts, it calls for the liberation of forces common to man and Nature, forces for which desire furnishes us the closest image. To classicism and separation, Breton prefers romanticism and synthesis. Rapt hope in the future, interpretation of the marvelous as sign of a beyond nevertheless human, desire to recover the past, concern to lift all prohibitions in order to attain "the life of presence, nothing but presence," [130] hope of changing the world by liberating desire—such are the motifs which lead him to condemn the writers who speak of asceticism or dualism and to cherish those who promise the reconciliation of man with the World and with himself, restoring to language and to articulation their original power.

But this reconciliation was also the great concern of Hegel. Hegel dreamed of an absolute Knowledge, which art and religion announce and prepare and in which spirit, revealing that it is all, is perceived as the common source of Nature, man, and the history of men. Here all contradictions would be surmounted, all oppositions overcome. Nevertheless, we do not believe Breton's project is the same as Hegel's and it appears that the confusion of these two projects—partly responsible for the obstinacy of surrealists in declaring themselves partisans of Marxist dialectic—has done the greatest disservice for surrealism. Breton has many times affirmed his admiration for Hegel. And without a doubt many of Hegel's formulas, dealing with the dialectical synthesis and the identity of contradictories, have managed to seduce him, appearing to him to explain his own poetic demands. Further, careful not to betray the cause of proletarian emancipation but obliged to react against the simplifications of Marxism and the neopositivist scientism miscalled "dialectical materialism," Breton was led to underline the Hegelian structure of Marx's analyses, to clarify and valorize Marx by Hegel. But did Breton in that way deepen his own intuition, or did he at least find a kindred spirit? I do not think so. It is the rights of the individual man that Breton feels it necessary to affirm and maintain, it is by a sort of nonconceptual evidence that he perceives their worth. In its "Political Position" surrealism will render homage to "the individual faculty that sends out a gleam in the great ignorance, in the great collective darkness," [131] and since the *Manifesto* Breton seems to envy fools for appreciating "their delirium enough to support the fact that it is valuable only for them." [132] Who cannot see in this the very definition of what Hegel condemns? Hegel always prefers history to the individual, prefers discursive language to intuitive evidence, universal verity to personal certitude. And it is in him that we find, alas, the first source of this contempt for man that we deplore today in so many Marxists. No doubt to understand Hegel's philosophy we must stop reducing it to its strictly explicit content; more than by the letter of its conceptual affirmations, a doctrine acts and imposes itself by steps and profound structures of which the author himself was not always conscious and which sometimes show up with clarity only in the practical or historical consequences of his thought. Wolfgang Paalen, in any case, was not mistaken in answering the queston "Will you admit Hegel?" with, "No, for his philosophy permits the justification of all the totalitarian régimes." [133]

Certainly, self-criticism in the name of norms foreign to consciousness and the organization of trials where the accused confesses and confounds his statements with those of his accusers—forgetting all intuitive certitude, all interior truth, every human ideal distinct from the order of the city—are part of a world specifically modern, none of whose horror Hegel foresaw. It must even be admitted that when he affirmed that Being is reducible to language and to universality, Hegel is doubtless concerned with delivering himself from his own solitude; here is manifest the terror of being right without everyone's approval, the passionate desire, like a panic, to be accepted by others, the concern to escape the essential sorrow of consciousness. But we know where this terror, this desire, this concern lead, or have led. Human and moving in origin, they always engender hideous and inhuman tyranny. For the rights of liberty are inseparable from the rights of solitude. By negating the value of solitude, Hegel destroys liberty; for him, to be right but against the World or History or Society is still to be wrong. An individual certitude, no matter what evidence produces it, cannot be a truth. The only possible basis for the true is, for Hegel, communications between consciousnesses; rational language is the unique principle of universal accord. In the name of "universal self-consciousness" Hegel rejects any appeal to sentiment, to intuition; he criticizes "die schöne Seele" that believes it has found in the depths of itself the divine absolute—he accuses it of madness and holds the properly moral exigency as abstract and formal. It is in morality, writes Breton on the contrary, "that I have always found my principal subjects for exaltation." [134] I have trouble, then, understanding why he has taken up in the *Second Manifesto* a sentence of Hegel declaring that "in the sphere of morality, inasmuch as it is distinguished from the social sphere, our convictions are only formal." [135] "The trial of the sufficiency of this formal conviction is no longer to be made," Breton adds, "and to wish at all cost to keep on with it is to the honor neither of the intelligence nor of the good faith of our contemporaries." Is not Breton's honor, even so, always to have preferred the formal moral conviction to the social conviction that Hegel calls "real conviction"? According to the norm set by the text of Hegel that Breton cites with praise, would we not in some disputes between Breton and the Communist party have to side with the latter? In any case, nothing is less Hegelian than this other phrase from the *Second Manifesto:* "There are yet throughout the world, in lycées, in studios even, in the street, in seminaries and casernes, young and pure beings who refuse the rut. It is only to those that I write..." [136] In this admirable appeal, where the individual affirms the totality of his rights and revolts against social constraint, no matter what name or face it borrows, we find the authentic voice of Breton, closer to those he denies than to those he claims. Never, in fact, has Breton subordinated the evidence of duty to the demands of the system; the universality to which he tends is therefore more Kantian than Hegelian. It sacrifices nothing, in any case, of interior certitude or of the value of the individual, and does not pretend to "conserve" them by "going past" them, according to the celebrated formulas of the dialectical mystification.

Breton's attachment to Hegel, reaffirmed in his recent *Entretiens,*[137] cannot, of course, rest on pure misunderstanding. It has first an emotional source in the reaction of the young Breton against the anti-Hegelian sarcasms of his philosophy professor, the positivist André Cresson. The titanesque and monstrous side of Hegel's work must also exercise on Breton a positive seduction. But, doubtless more profoundly, Breton could not but admire in Hegel the will to negate all transcendence or, which amounts to the same thing, to project all transcendence onto a horizontal plane. "The transformation of the old metaphysics into Logic," writes Hyppolite on Hegel, "signifies the negation of a transcendent being that reason could know, but would be an intelligible world before such a reason. *The absolute is subject,* and not substance; the Absolute is the speculative knowledge of Logic. *God is accessible only in pure speculative knowledge, and is only in this knowledge, and is only this knowledge itself.* Theology realized the intelligible beyond the intelligence. Hegelian logic knows neither thing-in-itself nor intelligible world. The Absolute does not think anywhere but in this phenomenal world; it is in our thought that the absolute thought thinks, that being manifests itself as thought and as sense . . ."[138] The desire, basic with Breton, to abolish religion without losing the religious exigency of man must then be satisfied here. It is not in fact in the eighteenth century, as scholars would like to convince us, but in the nineteenth that the coherent project of getting rid of religion and metaphysics forever was formed. This project could only develop by the divinization of history. In the eighteenth century, metaphysics and religion, denied from without, survived in their own originality. In Kant's "Transcendental Dialectic" the idea is formulated for the first time that the illusion inherent in them should rather be comprehended than refuted; still Kant never made of this comprehension a weapon against the liberty of the knowing subject. With Hegel, finally, who pretends to comprehend all the affirmations preceding his system into a larger truth which alone would give them their sense, all evidence separated from the individual judging subject is integrated into a cosmological dialectic, all personal consciousness is dissolved, every attempt by men to discover a transcendent principle of judgment, a truth superior to history, is condemned. The vertical dimension of man that the seventeenth century took so much care to preserve is negated. Still we must know whether such an enterprise realizes man wholly, allowing him his total powers, or if it robs him of the only freedom he can effectively attain. The affirmation of a transcendent principle of judgment, of a truth superior to history, permits revolt and resistance against the social; with Descartes, the contact of the individual spirit with the infinite gives basis at once for that spirit's certitude and its freedom. Negating the possibility of such an appeal, Hegel disarms the consciousness. In the prisons of the ancien régime the accused could at least rest on the authority of an intemporal absolute misunderstood by his judges. In the Hegelian prison, in the midst of a history whose achievement alone will constitute the Absolute, he can only prepare to admit before the law of the State that his solitary revolt and certitude were nothing but error and illusion.

I know Breton has always condemned transcendence and metaphysics. Even so, he seems to me to have been faithful to them in spirit. We must distrust the explicit content of the formulas; it reflects only a system of concepts, expression always approximate and abstract of a human attitude that itself remains basic. It is from experience that all affirmations borrow their value, it is the mental intention that furnishes content and weight to ideas. The ambivalence of tendencies is often contrasted with the precision of ideas, but, on the contrary, it is the idea which—isolated from its living context—remains ambivalent. Thus, the idea of the unified and total man in Hegel participates in the climate proper to the beginning of the nineteenth century, a reactionary and anti-individualistic climate which colors the not so Hegelian affirmations of De Maistre and of De Bonald. Here history and the city are queens, the individual claim is condemned; from the State and the Church man expects his salvation. Breton expects it only from man himself, from his desires and his delights. For him the basis of certitude is individual, the infinite rebels against the controls of a logical reason, will not be reduced to discursive language. That would be Cartesian, if Breton did not negate God. At least it is poetry and not system for which the Cartesian "meditation" makes way. Poetry carries the weight of all man's hope and gathers to itself the heritage of religion.

This is why Breton's project takes the form of a hope, irreducible but not rationally justified. For Hegel history is the field of language and the instrument of universality. For Breton it is in dreams and in his marvelous hopes that man is proclaimed. Poetry, far from seeking a place in a logic which would give it its sense, becomes alogical and confers a new sense on the World. Instead of waiting for the realization of its wishes from the unrolling of history or submitting to the point of finding greater riches in history than in its own dream, it ignores the round about way and opposes to the compromises of politics an evidence that sacrifices no desire. We might, therefore, say that it contains a sort of eternity; in any event it is hard to distinguish in it between will turned toward the future and regret, heavy with the past. It is indissolubly hopeful and nostalgic. "Not every paradise is lost," says the poem "Clair de terre." [139] In another, a little girl, "worshipper of the land traced on your perfumes," [140] makes us think of Baudelaire's desire to go live in "the land that resembles you." [141] And the first *Manifesto* declares, "The spirit that plunges into surrealism relives with exaltation the best part of its childhood. ... Perhaps childhood comes closest to real life ... childhood where everything concurs ... in the effective possession, and without hazards, of oneself." [142] Happiness here takes the form of a self-coincidence which alone permits what Breton calls belief, belief that precisely the temporal unrolling of life has been broken and we must recover its purity. "The belief in life, in the most precarious aspect of life—of real life—goes so far that in the end this faith is lost." [143] But "each morning children part without uneasiness. Everything is close by, the worst material conditions are excellent. The woods are white or black, we shall never sleep again." [144]

There is no need to underline the non-Hegelian character of such texts; they affirm the value of what Hegel called the immediate, what all Hegel's philosophy tried to show as radically poor, any richness arising, for Hegel, from mediation and belonging to the concept. Breton, it is true, never makes nostalgia an end in itself. He has even refused the Proustian remembrance of things past, though it too is dominated by the love of childhood and the sense of delight. But what separates Breton from Proust and keeps him from succumbing to a metaphysics of the eternal is assuredly not Hegelian logic. It is rather a Kantian concern with universality, the refusal to reserve to a few privileged persons this world of marvels which he wishes might become the world of all men. This is why Breton condemns aestheticism and, in love with childhood, never discusses his own childhood. We recount only ourselves, poetry is addressed to all and wishes to transform man. In the poetic experience Breton finds, even more than a presentiment of the future, a contact of individual and universal; and far from submitting to the system of history, the surrealist experience judges history by the norm of some eternity. "Surrealism," we read in *Médium*,[145] "is the encounter of the temporal aspect of the world with eternal values: love, liberty, and poetry." In this Breton's moral position remains more Cartesian than Hegelian. But it presupposes a tension difficult to maintain; we shall, therefore, see surrealism, in contact with difficulties and ordeals, often hesitate and sometimes contradict itself. Its hesitations and contradictions will be conceptual, however, and on the level merely of discourse. In spirit they will reveal the continuity of a unique exigence that surrealism has not gone back on. Unlike Hegel's disciples, Breton, refusing to let a state or a party judge in his place, maintains the solitary rights of a thought discovering in itself its first certitude. The truth that he announces is, by that, metaphysical, and it is no accident that the words sur-realism and meta-physics have the same structure. Certainly, the expository procedures of metaphysics and of surrealism differ entirely. But many philosophers having—after Hegel—rejoined the party of politicians and tyrants, giving themselves to the miserable task of justifying what is, no doubt it belonged to poetry to find again the sense of philosophy and to remind men of what should be.

Chapter Two
Revolt and Revolution

i. The Surrealist Refusal

Surrealist nihilism is a common phrase. "Absolute revolt,"
Camus writes, "total insubordination, sabotage the rule,
humor and worship of the absurd—surrealism in its first
intent may be defined as the trial of everything, always
beginning again." [1] The surrealists "believed they could
exalt murder and suicide." [2] "These frenetics wanted a
revolution of any sort, no matter what it took to free
them from the world of shopkeepers and compromises
they were forced to live in. Unable to have the best, they
preferred the worst. In this, they were nihilists." [3] If we
add here a bit of theology, nihilism becomes satanism.
According to Gengenbach, "it is certain that the surrealists joined with Lucifer." [4] And a priest, a friend of
Claude Mauriac, "having one day received from a too
well-intentioned gentleman a complete documentation
on surrealism ... had the impression of a direct envoy
from Hell." [5]

To tell the truth I am little qualified to pass on what
comes from Hell and what does not. But Claude Mauriac
remarks, very justly to my notion, that one "must believe
in Satan in order to dream of serving him," and that
"Breton has too much business with men to occupy himself with angels, even fallen ones." [6] Certainly, surrealism

has multiplied its insults against priests, the Church, and God himself. We have only to remember that the publication, in 1947, of *A la niche les glapisseurs de Dieu* recalls the violences of the beginnings of *La Révolution surréaliste*. But it is not sufficiently considered, in determining the sense of such insults, how the question of faith in God must be posed first. A blasphemy, we often hear, presupposes faith. This is a hasty judgment. To keep the literal and logical sense of a blasphemy we must, of course, suppose the existence of the one to whom it is addressed, namely God. But if the blasphemer has begun by declaring that he does not believe in God, we are forced to understand his remarks in another sense, and no longer invoke satanism. The apostrophes called blasphemous, the surrealists have said explicitly, "are obviously devoid in our eyes of any objective on the divine level, but . . . continue to express our irreducible aversion with respect to any being on his knees." [7] Let us recognize, consequently, that there is no point in searching here for the vertigo of a rebellious liberty, refusing to submit to a God whose existence is admitted. Surrealist blasphemy insults, not God, but believers. It seeks to overturn their consciousness, destroy in them a vain respect, an idea without object, to put in place of what the surrealists take for an error the truth of man and his reality, unique source of values. Thus, the theoretical denial of God precedes, with Breton, antireligion; it is the effect of a doubt rather than of a revolt. And one may, of course, think that in denying God Breton is mistaken. But we cannot claim that in blaspheming he takes the side of evil or of the void. Quite the contrary, he takes the side of Good and of Being, and on this point Claude Mauriac is right to state that Breton "loves only good and lives only for it." [8]

But, someone will reply, things are not so simple. The order of dependence between the theoretical negation of God and revolt against a God whose existence is accepted is not easy to determine; a first revolt may be the source of a theoretical negation, which then becomes passionate and in bad faith. As Carrouges remarks: "Sometimes in the guise of atheism there flourishes antitheism, that is, no longer the pure and simple absence of faith, but a furious conflict between faith and hatred toward God." [9] All this is perfectly true. But in order to resolve such questions in any particular case, it would be necessary to understand an author better than he understands himself; the critic for this has to become "Promethean" and take himself for God at the Judgment Day. With a slighter ambition, I should like to take the numerous texts in prophetic style that Carrouges has assembled to illustrate his theory of a literature dominated by the desire of man to take God's place and to distinguish between those issued from revolt and those engendered by a theoretical negation. The celebrated formula of Nietzsche, "God is dead, now we want the Superman to live," [10] can be taken in two contrary senses. And I do not quite understand how Carrouges can cite on the same page—and take as practically equivalent—Bakunin's sentence, "Even if God existed it would be necessary to suppress him," and that of Dostoevski, "If God is, all will belongs to him and outside of his will I can do nothing; if he is not, all will is mine and I must proclaim my own will." [11] In Bakunin's statement and in this of Georges Bataille also cited by Carrouges, "Is it God that I would like to have power to rend?" I manage to find no sense (the reader will excuse my lack of penetration into matters of satanism). As for the text of Dostoevski, I see hardly any means to contradict it; it enunciates, quite apart from Luciferian revolt, the two terms of a rational alternative. Breton has chosen the second. Believing that God is not, he supposes with perfectly good logic that all will belongs to man. An atheist cannot judge otherwise.

Thus, we must altogether separate surrealist atheism from romantic satanism, to which it has so often been linked. According to Carrouges, Breton makes "appeal to the powers of darkness," gathers "the notion of a primitive malediction," has recourse to "damned forces, human and superhuman" in order to attribute "a victorious power to the cosmic revolt," and sees in God "a Being of revenge and aggression." [12] The show of satanism, in spite of the affirmation (itself contradictory) of a possible victory for the cosmic revolt, can only be despair. If God exists, if he is the source of all reality, what can revolt against him in fact mean? It can only end in failure; for man, it consists in turning toward the void. Now one can hardly turn toward the void except by a pride which quickly drifts toward theatricalism. The Luciferian hero offers other men the vision of his dark silhouette descending into hell, like Don Giovanni in the last act, in an attitude of supreme defiance. But nothing is more foreign to the essence of surrealism than the idea of a beauty-as-spectacle, even black spectacle. The surrealist project comes from positive hope, it is effort at realization and impatience for being. If in fact God does not exist, it is no longer in an atmosphere of damnation and of blasphemy that we must think of the concrete revolution that will establish the world of the human. There is no question of undertaking a hopeless battle against Being, but of winning, which is completely different. Surrealism charges the idea of God with limiting man, of hindering him from essaying the conquest of all his powers. This is no satanism, but humanist confidence, that is, negation of any superiority of Being over man, affirmation that—every reality and every value being relative to man—man's enterprises cannot be restricted.[13] Humanism being first theoretically affirmed, the revolt against God is no longer the despairing revolt against Being, but revolt against the illusions which, according to Breton, hinder man's attaining to being. Once again, one may decide that Breton is wrong. But the spirit animating him is that of love, of hope, and of confidence in our freedom.

We must not neglect, nevertheless, the many surrealist

texts that justify Carrouges' interpretation, and Breton's taste for black and nihilistic images. When, in *L'Amour fou,* Breton writes, "Love, only love there is, carnal love," we may hope at first that in the name of a humanism clearly accepted he is going to inveigh against all the prohibitions of a sexual code made up of prejudices. But he adds, "I adore, I have never ceased to adore, your venomous shadow, your deathly shadow." And the following sentence, "A day will come when man will recognize you as his only lord and honor you even unto the mysterious perversions that are your entourage," [14] might well pass for Satanic and consequently locate itself in a logic that in spite of itself leads back toward the religion that Breton pretends to combat. If the shadow of carnal love is venomous and deathly, can one find Life other than in divine love? The hope, formulated by Breton in *Point du jour,* that not the dove "but the crow" should return [15] and the affirmation of *Arcane 17* (where he nevertheless sings "life in what life has most inviting" [16]) by which Lucifer is the father of "poetry and freedom" [17] could lead a rigorous mind to similar conclusions. How interpret these texts, without being content to see them as simple literary exercises with no import? Gracq, who has rightly shown that the word "black" (in black novel, black museum, black washhouse, black diamond, black god, etc.), "by relation to the Luciferian attraction, polarizes negatively all the magnetic fields over which Breton's flag floats," supposes that this word "gathers for the surrealists all the galvanic charge we see it capable of" by reference to "sacrilege" and to "profanation." [18] But sacrilege presupposes faith. How reconcile that with the incontestably positive hope and the morality of the surrealist consciousness, morality that may be maintained only to the extent that God is theoretically denied.

The answer cannot be simple. I believe that to explain the apparent nihilism of Breton, it is first necessary to take into account the influences exterior to surrealism proper, the ballast that surrealism has carried from its beginnings. The prestige of German romanticism and the experience, totally negative, of the Dada movement join here with the interiorization of Vaché, in whom the sentiment of failure seemed to dominate. Victor Crastre has made the opposition of Vaché and surrealism precise, in definitive sentences: "Surrealism opens a large credit for man; Vaché denies him the slightest. Surrealism engages the future, even the most distant; Vaché considers only the present, he has killed the future by killing himself. Finally, surrealism finds an open door in mystery; Vaché, on the contrary, closes all doors." [19] Still, Breton has written, "Vaché is surrealist in me." [20] And Gracq, commenting on this sentence, suggests that what was "best" in the spirit of Vaché "literally went through" Breton (as did the best in Sade's spirit, Lautréamont's, Jarry's, etc.).[21] There is no doubt that Vaché's spirit "went through" Breton and held him in its power. On the other hand one may ask if, even in Breton, Vaché managed to become surrealist. Vaché furnished Breton a certain number of images which Breton himself has some trouble expounding. The incident at the premiere of *Les Mamelles de Tirésias*,[22] when Vaché entered the hall with a revolver, is no doubt the source of the celebrated statement in the *Second Manifesto:* "The simplest surrealist act consists in going, revolver in hand, into the street and firing as much as possible at random into the crowd." [23] This sentence has, of course, been too much quoted, and fools have remembered only it. The fact remains that Breton wrote it, and it is hard to connect with his marvelous hope. In fact each time the influence of Vaché makes itself felt, Breton seems to undergo an interior duel and something analogous to possession; the dialogue between the ecstatic poet and the negator who in 1916 made fun of his literary admirations is carried on in Breton himself for a long time after Vaché's death. The tendency that inspired *Poisson soluble* is placed against a bitter and deprecating irony. The strange text in *Les Pas perdus* called "Jacques

Vaché"[24] seems to illustrate this combat better than any other; the results of automatism are still positive, but the abrupt rhythm involves a sort of negation that continually goes against the inspiration. And in the pages of *"the disdainful confession,"* also consecrated to Jacques Vaché, the enthusiasm and the curiosity "passionately exercised on beings"[25] always find their counterpart in some deception. "What truth can there be if there is death?" Breton asks himself, following Tolstoi. And he resists adapting his existence "to the ridiculous conditions, here below, of all existence."[26] "This is why," he concludes, "everything that may be realized in the intellectual realm always appears to me to witness to the worst servility or the most complete bad faith. I love, it is true, only unaccomplished things."[27]

But nothing is completely explained by influences. Vaché would not at this point have made an impression on Breton if revolt had not had in Breton some accent of despair. And one must not forget the profound discouragement that often possessed the surrealists. If it was more obvious in some few and led Crevel in 1935 to suicide, it had its hand on all. The first number of *La Révolution surréaliste*[28] notes all the cases of suicide reported in the newspapers over a certain period and opens the famous inquiry: is suicide a solution? The declaration of January 27, 1925, rather contradictory in other respects, speaks of the "altogether despairing" character of the revolution undertaken.[29] "Of taste I know only distaste," writes Pierre Naville in the third number of *La Révolution surréaliste.*[30] And Breton, taking over the editorship from the fourth number, recalls "the original justification of the surrealist cause" and returns to a positive hope: "We want and we will have the beyond of our days. For that, it is enough to listen only to our impatience and wait without reticence for orders from the marvelous."[31] But in the same number, the tone of Aragon is quite different: "I curse science. . . . We are the defeatists of Europe. . . . We will wake everywhere the germs of confusion and malaise.... We are those who will always give a hand to the enemy." [32] What is this force of pure negation that in the surrealist consciousness opposes the positive hope of humanism and the ecstasy of marvelous love?

I think we cannot deny the element of confused culpability that from the beginning is found linked to the surrealist refusal. And no doubt such an element is present in any passionate revolt. Must we add: in any revolt, no matter what? I do not think so. A revolt that would be unswerving but motivated in perfect clarity seems possible to me, a revolt of reason itself (I mean Kant's "practical reason") against a state of things it judges evil. But in total revolt and also in the revolutionary consciousness that the surrealists make theirs, there are necessarily mixed creation and destruction, love and hate, jealousy and a sense of justice, generosity and cruelty; revolt cannot then altogether be justified, be brought into the light or be consistent with itself— it can only be lived. Far from believing that, as some political propaganda invites us to believe, in a conflict of men all the right may be on one side and all the evil on the other, far from justifying this foolishness, as sometimes people try more perfidiously to do in consideration of some higher interest or of the future of history, an interest or future supposedly known to the heads of an army or a movement whose discipline it then suffices to follow, we must avow that all revolt is—to say the least—moral risk, and the images that nourish it trouble us so deeply only because they are themselves fundamentally troubled. The moral risk of effectively destructive revolt cannot, no matter what hoaxers say, rationally be made legitimate; the risk can be run, can be accepted, in fact, only by grace of passion. So Breton has declared, "Once emptied of its content of passion, what is left of revolt?" [33] Actually, the surrealist revolt, if moral in its essence, is presented often as a sort of sacred fury. The text of April 2, 1925, signed by Artaud, Boiffard, Leiris, Masson, and Naville, is characteristic in this respect; the signers state that "before any surrealist or revolutionary preoccupation, what dominates their spirit is a certain state of fury" and that "it is along the path of this fury that they are most likely to attain what one might call surrealist illumination." [34] The basis of the surrealist refusal is affective and lived, it is a protest of man as a whole, a decision to destroy what constrains and limits him.

But any fury in man feels itself obscurely guilty and risks being turned against itself. There is only one step from fury to suicide. Fury lets an essential ambivalence appear, and in it we find again, by a strange but necessary reversal, the dualism that surrealism at its beginning tried to evade. Surrealism affirms the unity of spirit and desire; it refuses to dissociate man, it opposes the world with a revolt springing from the totality of being. Since reason sometimes goes contrary to desire, it disqualifies reason, confounding it with the objects fit to revolt against, challenging it with spirit (according to Crevel's title, *L'Esprit contre la raison*).[35] Never in all this does reflection manage to continue at the source or to become the measure of revolt. And I think that in many a case this attitude has hindered the surrealists from perceiving the authority of their revolt itself, from realizing its possible justification. For after all, in revolting against reason the surrealists were most often on the reasonable side. Thus, Breton was right in thinking that no philosopher and no poet had taken the necessary line in regard to the war, that no French intellectual between 1914 and 1918 had been up to the level of what was taking place. And the disappointment he felt before this deficiency and which was expressed, for example, in 1921 by the "indictment of Barrès" was rational and even reasonable. But reasonable disappointment leaves room for fury in all the manifestations that mark the beginning of the surrealist movement: the insults to Madame Aurel at the Polti banquet, attacks on Anatole France in the publi-

cation of *Un Cadavre,* the letter to Claudel, the dis-
turbances at the Saint-Pol-Roux banquet. In each of these
affairs, when the surrealists express their disgust and
hatred for all that seems sacred to the society in which
they live, there is no doubt that their intention remains
moral. Recalling the insults addressed to "family,"
"country," "religion," and even to "labor" and to "honor,"
Breton writes, "Our spirits were very aware of the human
sacrifices the gods had demanded, and were demanding
again." [36] "The world," he adds, "scandalized us." [37] But
surrealism attempts no rational criticism of this world
like that with which Voltaire opposed fanaticism (which
likewise scandalized him). The surrealists put themselves
"into a posture of aggression." [38] "Certain words of
Lautréamont, of Rimbaud," Breton writes, "of an im-
perious character, detached themselves from their message as if in letters of fire. They constituted for us veritable countersigns and we meant not to delay in their
execution." [39]

Without a doubt it is Artaud who lived with most
violence the fury of refusal that possessed the group.
All, however, accept the violence of the scandal and its
illumination. Alone, passion realizes the unity of desire
and spirit. But from this fact, revolt is accompanied by
some obscure doubt as to its legitimacy and is thus divided against itself. How can a movement of the spirit
know if it heads toward good or evil, once the light of
reason is outlawed and the distinctions of the understanding are rejected? Even if God is denied, has man
all rights? Does not the very ambition of his limitless desire condemn it to failure? Unformulated, these questions
crowd into the background of the texts of "scandal"
from the first period. The doubt they introduce begins,
after its fashion, to dissociate the unity of man. And
such interrogations will always maintain in surrealism
an essential ambiguity. Thus, in what concerns the liberation of sexual taboos (an area in which reason should
suffice to conquer prejudice) Breton, after having spoken

in *L'Amour fou* of the venomous and deadly shadow of carnal love that he nevertheless adores, adds, "I have not yet succeeded in obtaining from the genius of beauty that it might be altogether the same with its bright wings or its dark wings. . . . The child that I remain in comparison with all I should like to be has not quite unlearned the dualism of good and evil." [40] A particularly enlightening text, for in it childhood is not taken as the paradise we must regain but is considered the obstacle to this true synthesis Breton perceives, perhaps for the first time, cannot be discovered in an affectivity always ready to divide against itself, but in the beyond of a reconciliation for which only reason can furnish us the presentiment.

Guilt, even confused, quickly becomes fear; it evokes then, by the idea of possible punishment, knowledge—and reminds us that we are mortal. The image of the black hero returns to haunt the hope of the surrealists and with it the fear, sometimes panic, which Leiris tells us, movingly and sincerely, hardly ever left him throughout the period of the scandals.[41] The surrealist consciousness is enlarged in this way by a dramatic dimension. Is it necessary to recall that it wanted never to renounce anything and that one of the concerns of surrealism was to continue the battle against religion that the eighteenth century had essayed, without, for all that, accepting the Voltairean limitation of man to a sceptical and desiccated reason? Wishing to regain the whole of man, including whatever was authentic in his religious emotion, surrealism recovers, without believing in God, the vertigo of facing evil. Inevitably then, it encountered the eighteenth-century man whose extraordinary merit was putting naturalist hopes before his responsibilities: the marquis de Sade. In him the violence against society, against religion, and against the world recovers its primary source in the deepest layers of desire and the most purely natural. But by the same stroke it is clear that there can be no order in desire. For desire is violence, it transforms others into means. It may, indifferently and by chances beyond reasonable control, find an excitement in their suffering or pleasure in provoking their suffering; it may exasperate them and attain a sort of firmament of enjoyment at their torture and agony. No one has revealed more clearly than Sade the ambivalence of sentiment and the ambiguity of this idea of human nature, which so many spirits of his century acquired so easily. But no one is more obscure than Sade the moralist. What does he mean? What advice is he giving us? He uses the words "vicious" and "villain" sometimes as praise, sometimes as blame. He recognizes no god but voluptuousness, but always associates it with some crime. I have no intention, certainly, of trying to explain Sade, and I am far from having arrived at a definitive opinion of him. But one must admit that with Sade human desire attains self-consciousness with a lucidity and a freedom that his century hardly knew. It is no doubt difficult to decide whether Sade takes the side of order or that of instinct; in any case he teaches that man's instincts can be completely satisfied only in derangement and comes round in his fashion to the Kantian truth that there is not and cannot be an ethics of sentiment or an order in passion. And I never think without emotion of Sade's courage during the Terror in speaking out against the death penalty, when the disciples of Rousseau and good Dame Nature were chopping off heads in the name of virtue. Here it strikes us that Sade's inhuman message doubtless contained a deeper humanity than all the speeches of debonair philanthropy. But no one yet can flatter himself that he has found the key to the message, and the surrealists searching like Sade for the sense of revolt in the intensity of desire have lived Sade's truth more than they have understood it.

Breton, it is true, always insisted on the contribution of Sade's writings to man's grasp of consciousness. "What was needed," he says in regard to Sade, "in order to define the fundamental aspirations of this thought was nothing less than the will shown by true analysts to extend, surmounting all prejudices, the field of human knowledge." [42] But instead of trying theoretically to explicate the sense of Sade's work, surrealism has preferred to urge us to read him and to present us with the spectacle of cruel acts and thus to enlarge the sense of what we are, simply by troubling the emotion then fostered in us. Thus, in the film *L'Age d'or* by Buñuel and Dali we see the hero, before being reunited with the woman he loves, knock over a blind man with a violent kick. What does this image mean? It is clear that we are not being advised to strike the blind, as I think some fools have supposed. But it is equally clear that we have not been offered a spectacle merely aesthetically overwhelming or disconcerting. All laborious discursive commentary, such as would reveal the implicit condemnation of a pity always egocentric and hypocritical, must also be rejected; this is not a matter of redoing the *Maximes* of La Rochefoucauld. What then is the point of our being inflicted with this emotion, of which we only feel that it collaborates, not without violence, in our grasp of our own consciousness, that it concurs in this exploration, in the spirit's recuperation of all its powers that remains the essential end of surrealism? The surrealists do not tell us clearly whether they approve or disapprove of the properly sadistic act. They make us partake by giving it a value, its troubling temptation; they make us live a totally pure revolt, revolt in the face of life, in face of the very conditions of existence, before everything that constrains desire and love.

The surrealists adopt an analogous attitude toward Lautréamont, that other Sade, who also disappeared behind a work shot through by the derangement of cruelty and the vertigo of crime. Breton writes, "The time is not ripe for a study of the moral scope of the work of Ducasse." [43] He limits himself to remarking that this work "inflicts a tropical climate on the sensibilities," expresses a "total revelation that seems to exceed human possibilities." To picture Lautréamont, he tries to recover the contradictory colors which served Swinburne in drawing Sade, "This cloaca is all bursting with azure." "The terms madness, proof by absurdity, infernal machine," says Breton again, "that have been used, indeed reused, in regard to this work show that criticism never approaches it without sooner or later sounding a retreat." [44] One could not better express how the sense of Sade's work or Lautréamont's cannot be put into precepts. But we see what a step the discovery of these works makes us take, at what distance they take us from the simple hope of happiness we still believe remains the basis of surrealism, the hope that *Poisson soluble* revealed in all its purity. Can we, after reading Sade and Lautréamont, say with the Breton of *Poisson soluble,* "Ah! but parallels are beautiful under God's perpendicular," [45] or again, "Near to God the sketchbook of this castle was open to a drawing of shade, feathers, iris"? [46] "Now," wrote Breton, "is the sweetness that recovers the boulevard, like a salt-marsh under luminous ensigns . . ." "Servants of weakness, servants of happiness, women take advantage of light in bursts of laughter." [47] But Sade teaches us that the desire that makes us see women as possible "servants of happiness" may, if we give ourselves to it, make them tortured slaves of pleasure. And *Les Chants de Maldoror* reinforces this vertigo. There the essential violence of Nature is revealed, the infinity of human need, the battle of one consciousness with another, the insoluble drama of passion. The total man, desirous and impassioned, appears almost unbearably tense and as though split between his divinization and his annihilation. His refusal will thus be torn between the dimension of the real and that of the imaginary. This division, the oscillation between the two terms, the despairing hope of their reunion in the future, will be at once an essential energy in the development of surrealism and the tragic source of its hesitations.

II. Surrealism and Marxism

"Marx said, 'Transform the world'; Rimbaud said, 'Change life'; these two mottoes are for us one and the same." [48] This is the last sentence in the lecture Breton should have given (and was prevented from giving) at the Congress of Revolutionary Writers held in Paris in June 1935. And in his dialogue with Aimé Patri about Camus' *L'Homme révolté*,[49] Breton states that "the whole psychological approach of surrealism was directed" by such a "concern for unification." Breton thus affirms as the object of his essential will the realization of man's unity by the meeting of two opposed paths where our desire is engaged: that of the imaginary, of poetry, perhaps of madness; that of science, of practical activity, of political realization. But wanting, even with all one's might, to unify these two paths is not necessarily to succeed in their unification or even to demonstrate its possibility. Has the surrealist will other reasons for confidence than what it might discover in desire itself, in the human demand that like its own is at the basis of Rimbaud's approach and also of Marx's? Surrealism wishes to remain faithful to the whole of this initial desire, already contradictory and strained. Can it, however, follow the two opposing paths to which it engages us? Indeed, the aim of Marxism and the aim of surrealist poetry are the same: man's liberation. But Breton himself says, "To my mind the aim of anything is less what it claims to be than what the means it uses make it." [50] Now the means that desire employs to gain its ends differ fundamentally according to whether it bows or does not bow to reason. In the celebrated dictum of Bacon, "Nature to be commanded must be obeyed." Such is the path of technology; it presupposes patience, it delays enjoyment of its goal, it accepts adaptation to the necessity of things, it attempts to learn these necessities, and its action is modeled according to their structure. We recognize here the nature of labor and of politics and we understand why Marxism, a political theory, would see in labor the basic relation between man and Nature. But desire may take another route, that of the imaginary. It then derealizes this world, forgets its laws, and is satisfied in changing our very manner of apprehending it. This is the path of emotion, of dream, of reverie, of poetry, and of madness. The opposition of the two paths creates in surrealism a painful tension between the political exigency of effective action and the exigency of total liberation from all restraints. For if there are men who came to the revolution by reflecting on history or economics, Breton is not one of them. His point of departure is pure revolt, violent emotion and, as he puts it, "the letting go, the exaltation and the pride" that, while still a child, "the discovery" in a cemetery he had been brought to "of a simple granite stone engraved in red capitals with the superb device: NOR GOD NOR MASTER" had granted him.[51] He chose the red flag long ago, but continues "to tremble still more" when the black flag is evoked.[52] "Open the prisons, let the army go," said the second number of *La Révolution surréaliste*. "And war against labor," the fourth number added.[53] One of the justifications of automatic writing given in 1933 will still be the refusal to "correct" or to "correct oneself," [54] and thus the rejection of all constraint and all order.

Still, I do not believe that Marxist surrealism succumbed to this particular tension. Of the split between surrealists and communists, the facile explanation that action is incompatible with a revolt leading toward the escape of dream has too often been proposed. This is forgetting that the surrealist affirmation of the deep unity of dream and action by no means signifies the pure and simple reduction of action to dream. It neglects the admirable and untiring efforts of the surrealists toward efficacy and underestimates the revolutionary will that, for example, sent Benjamin Péret to fight in

Spain. In fact, if there had existed at the time a party both revolutionary and nontotalitarian, I mean one not presuming to dictate all the forms of spiritual activity, surrealism would assuredly have found its place therein. In any case the surrealists always sought avidly for such a party, as the encounters of Breton and Trotsky [55] and the nostalgia in the *Ode à Charles Fourier* testify.[56] *Arcane 17* evokes with regret the time when "all sorts of lacerations inside the proletariat had not yet come about," [57] and we may state that it was not Breton's fault if a properly political activity was always impossible for him. No, Breton did not flee before the difficulties that real life opposed to his hope of the marvelous. If he maintained, against certain Marxists, that between man and Nature there are other basic relations besides labor, he has not mistaken the alienation of man in a labor whose fruits are denied him and which transforms him into a thing. But other discords—and irreducible ones—remained between the philosophy implicit in surrealism and the Marxist doctrine. Surrealism believes in freedom of spirit. "Among so many disgraces that are our heritage," says the *Manifesto*, "we must recognize that the greatest freedom of spirit is still ours." [58] Descartes found proof of our liberty in our experience of it; Breton discovers proof of the liberty of his spirit in his very revolt. Does not the fact that man judges matter and history prove that his spirit is superior to matter and to history? Here again we find as the first and necessary condition of the spirit's emancipation the surrealist negation of any reality that is able—from without and having no consciousness of the process—to constrain the spirit. Just as he refused the transcendence of God, Breton refuses that of Matter, of History, of Society, of any *an sich* set up as radically anterior to consciousness and rendering consciousness a slave. Thus, he cannot admit, even in the problematical hope of a spiritual liberation deferred to the end of time, the primacy of matter dogmatically affirmed by the Marxists or the complete ex-

planation of an individual and his thought by reference
to history and society. On this subject, *Rupture inaugurale,* a text signed in 1947 by members of the new
surrealist group, contains a moot critique of historical
materialism and demonstrates the independence, at least
relative, of the life of thought in its relation to economic
conditioning. "The moral doctrine of Christianity, sanc-
tioned in all civilized countries by a common and constant profane law, is expressed in the Decalogue, which
remains the essence of the Mosaic revelation. The Marxists should deduce from this that there has been no
important change in the area of economics since Moses
was summoned to Mount Sinai. Aristotle's logic—to
leave the area of manners—is no longer that of Heraclitus, but is still that of Kant. Will the Marxists deduce
from this that between Heraclitus and Aristotle there
were economic modifications more important than between Aristotle and Kant?" [59] In this, the principles of
surrealist and of Marxist thought differ radically. And it
is enough to consider the first contacts of the surrealists
with the communists to see the incompatibility. In *La
Révolution d'abord et toujours* [60] these are still simultaneously affirmed: "We declare ourselves in insurrection
against history," the signers say, claiming in effect a
freedom traced from their "deepest spiritual necessities."
But elsewhere they write, "We are not Utopians; we
conceive this Revolution only in its social form." As a
matter of fact the groups that joined to sign this manifesto (*La Révolution surréaliste, Clarté, Philosophies,
Correspondance*) [61] did not hesitate in acknowledging
their divergences. Breton maintains, in the midst of the
union he desires, the proper autonomy of surrealism,
whose legitimacy the communists already contest. Then,
Naville wishes to force the surrealists to choose, and
fears that their encounter with the proletariat is acciden-
tal. "Surrealism," he writes, "when it praises 'the life
of dream, of the Oriental spirit considered as contemplation . . .' gets sidetracked, apparently guided by moral

principles, into a direction that from one moment to the next could put it into contradiction with the most elementary necessities of the proletarian revolution." [62] Naville, alluding here to the hope in the Orient that Breton has often expressed and which inspired numerous surrealist texts, such as the "Address to the Dalai-Lama" or the "Letter to the Buddhist Schools," [63] attempts no doubt wrongly to enclose surrealism in something that manifests it only partly. The basis of his criticism remains none the less valuable from a strictly materialist point of view. According to historical materialism, in effect, only the material transformation of society can produce forms of thought that are presently impossible to anticipate or describe. Revolution becomes then necessarily man's only task. It is clear that Breton has never accepted this view; revolution is for him only one of man's tasks—a task that derives its sense only in the light of its end, which must be thought or felt independently of means to attain it. And this end, if it cannot be the object of a really positive comprehension for us, may be already discovered and conceived as part of the exigency of human desire and of the experience of our freedom. And Breton, wanting to do justice to the hostility of the communists in 1926, writes in "Légitime défense," "No one among us does not wish the passage of power from the hands of the bourgeoisie to those of the proletariat. In the meantime, it is none the less necessary, we claim, for the experience of the interior life to continue and to continue, let it be understood, without exterior control, even Marxist." [64]

Thus, a revealing dialogue commences between surrealism and communism; we cannot speak of simple conflict, since at least for a long time the surrealists were declared friends with the Communist party, to which, in 1927, Aragon, Breton, Eluard, Péret and Unik belonged. Nor can we speak of deep accord; in the same 1927 the brochure *Au grand jour* brought out the differences that would later be aggravated and bring about the rupture of Breton with those of his old friends who would remain or return to the Communist party. In fact, the oscillating tension that at once attracts and separates surrealists and communists is internal to Marxism itself—this being why we should not say hastily, as has often been done, that surrealism, essentially foreign to Marxism, crossed the path of Marxism and then left it. The labors of Maximilien Rubel have established that Marx adhered to socialism before having constructed a materialist philosophy, in the name of a properly ethical exigency. "In the Marxist teaching," Rubel writes, "is a pathetic appeal to the individual whoever he may be, to the human in man, an appeal in which there is nothing doctrinal or speculative, but an ethical demand, an exhortation to total change both internal and visible." [65] In this sense we may say that the point of departure for Marx and for Breton was the same. But Marx constructed a historical and economic doctrine, which, one may fear, is incompatible with the affirmation of the legitimacy of the very exigency that was its origin and justification. In any case, if, like Rubel, we can hold that with Marx himself the ethical exigency and the system are compatible (which for myself I am not convinced of), the "Marxism" which follows Marx seems, by the logic of its materialist postulates, absolute rebel to any properly moral or metaphysical dimension. Thus those who like Breton are attracted to Marxism by the ethical demand are put in a position quite different from the one which confronted Marx. They find a doctrine already constituted, defended, or maintained by powerful and tyrannical organizations which have codified their answers on all philosophical questions and thus demand of the intellectual who desires to participate in their effort nothing less than utter abandonment of his own ideas and of any spirit of inquiry. We may reproach Breton for having between 1928 and 1932 taken the part of these organizations against himself, for having accepted, in order not to break with them, many of the theoretical propositions of "dialectical materialism" that had nothing to do with his own thought or with truth, and for having shown severity toward those who continued to say that the social liberation of man interested them less than did emancipation of the spirit. But how fail to recognize his tragic situation? To leave the Marxists altogether seemed to him to renounce the realization of his project for the effective liberation of man, to sacrifice efficacy and return to art as a refuge. To submit to the orders of the Communist party was to stop searching and to repeat passively the words of those who, it seemed, had found. So we see surrealism in the years after 1928, trying to submit to the communists who still appeared to be the only organization effectively fighting for the transformation of the material condition of men and at the same time developing—as a sort of antidote—a taste for adventure and pure research. *Nadja, Le Grand Jeu, Et les seins mouraient, Traité du style* in 1928, *L'amour, la poésie, La Grande gaieté* in 1929, and *Ralentir travaux, Artine, L'Immaculée conception* in 1930 show the desire for spiritual freedom in Breton, Char, Aragon, and Eluard resisting the suffocation of materialistic dogmatism. The tension becomes no less unbearable: soon each would have to choose. In 1935 the rupture between surrealism and the Communist party was to be made definitive.[66]

The drama Breton and his friends lived out is not peculiar to the surrealists. It is that of all intellectuals either communist or tempted by communism. The general analysis of its conditions would draw us from our subject. But it is important to remember that this drama is not from a conflict of action and dream, as some have claimed, nor as the communists have declared from the opposition of revolutionary will and desire for social conservatism. For no one as far as I know has established reasonably any connection between the Cartesian cogito, the Kantian analysis, or free creation in painting—all condemned by the communists—and dream or political

reaction; just as no one has shown how the platitudes
of aesthetic realism or the mediocrity of the philosophy
expatiated in *La Pensée* or *La Nouvelle critique* serve
the cause of the proletariat. The drama of the intellectual
attracted to communist politics really rises from the incompatibility between the internal evidences asserted in
him as in any man, moving his thoughts freely and
sincerely, and an external pat doctrine contrary to these
evidences, in which he cannot even see how its errors
are useful to the political and economic cause they pretend to serve. The history of this drama, the analysis
of the hesitations it has provoked, the recital of sufferings
it has engendered have not yet been seriously attempted.
Those prey to such lacerations (and this is within the
Communist party) in fact prefer to condemn one another,
rather than recognize their community of anxiety. So
Dionys Mascolo addresses the present surrealists with
criticisms it would seem he should address to himself,
since as Breton remarks, Mascolo's conclusions and those
of the surrealists concerning art and the revolution are
strictly identical.[67] But doubtless in this area many condemn publicly in others what they themselves accept
as true in the secrecy of their own hearts. The courage
of the surrealists, their impartiality, and their acceptance
of solitude appear once again as rare and exemplary.
Revolutionaries, the surrealists refuse to forget for an
instant the ends of the revolution and judge every enterprise by its ends. Does someone say that labor is the
fundamental relation between man and Nature? The
surrealists recall the irrepressible demand of their consciousness which is and wishes to be ecstatic; they therefore affirm that the true aim of labor is to free man from
labor and to lead him to the values of knowledge, of
contemplation, and of pleasure. Does someone, as is
today unfortunately fashionable, transplant the holy into
politics? The surrealists, who thanks to poetry retain
intact the sense of human totality, reject this degrading
mutilation. Their desire, in which dwell all grandeur

and all man's appetite, always surpasses the limited objectives to which people pretend to reduce it.

Thus, without wanting to, without perhaps knowing it, surrealism takes on itself the task which was always that of philosophy. Contrary to Hegel, who loses philosophy by wanting to make it into history's consciousness of itself, surrealism subordinates history to a consciousness capable of judging history. When Breton declares that consciousness has rights that cannot be regulated, that truth must not be effaced before efficacy, that the end does not justify the means, in effect he enunciates judgments whose final basis can be found only in the affirmation of the infinity of spirit, of its superiority over any possible object and over any definable concept. That affirmation is no other than the Cartesian cogito. And far from ceasing to be revolutionary Breton thus gives to the idea of revolution its only possible foundation, for the very idea of revolution presupposes the vertical dimension whereby the spirit, refusing to coincide with factual history, judges it, surpasses it, affirms that the actual state of things is inadmissable, and declares that the revolution is a good. In rejecting this transcendence of the spirit one can only end up adoring what is. The communists have not failed to do this, and Breton perfectly well sees it: "Can one ask us in advance," he writes, "to throw away this unlimited capacity of refusal that is the whole secret of human movement in order to leave us to the wonder of something happening at the other end of the earth?" [68] But, for all that, Breton does not go back to Descartes or Kant. His evidences are not in fact philosophical but artistic. What makes him indignant is not the caricature the communists present of the great philosophers before loading them with insults, but the dismaying texts in *Komsomolskaya Pravda*,[69] the "subjects prescribed for painters by the Hungarian minister of Culture" ("The Heroes of Labor Seated in Their Box at the Theater," "The First Tractor Arrives in the Village," "A Policewoman Helping a Child to Cross the Street," etc.),[70] "the ineptitude, multiplied by the raving need to suspect and to denounce" that Soviet art critics exhibit,[71] the nullity of the praised works, the lamentable proclamations of Zamushkin ("Cézanne is to be condemned, Matisse does not know how to draw, Picasso is putrid," etc.),[72] finally the attitude of Picasso and Matisse themselves "when they guarantee with their names an enterprise demanding the deathblow for the artistic consciousness and artistic freedom which had been the whole justification of their lives." [73] Everyone discovers truth in his own way; Breton's way is brightened less by metaphysical reflection than by the sentiment of beauty. It is none the less faithful to metaphysical truth.

But this way can only be one of tension and strife. Compelled to return to the idea of the importance of form and technique in art, to affirm the autonomy of art, its independence from history and thus to some extent its eternity, to recognize that for example in the case of Courbet or Rimbaud, before as after the Commune, "the great themes offered the poet and the artist continue to be the flight of the seasons, nature, woman, love, dream, life, and death," [74] Breton is for all that unresolved on separating entirely the cause of art and the cause of revolution. He is convinced that art may be used like a "weapon that in the decline of bourgeois society turns inevitably against that society." [75] He exalts "annunciatory" works that "by rapport with the historical circumstances that have unleashed them" take on the "semblance of a ship's figurehead." [76] Why does it have to be then that the bourgeoisie, which Breton detests, often receives favorably artistic innovation, while the officials of communism appreciate only paintings in all points similar to those of the academic artists at the end of the last century or poems that Déroulède and François Coppée themselves would have been embarrassed to show? Is there no connection between the will to social revolution and the will to cultural revolution? Does

there not exist, Breton asks, "an art that is in a position
to justify its advanced technique by the very fact that
it is in the service of a leftist state of spirit? Is it vain
to wish to discover between this state of spirit and that
technique a relation of cause to effect?" [77] And Breton
reflects on the comparison of David, official painter for
the French Revolution but whose art is deplorably academic, and Courbet, as revolutionary in politics as in
painting but who consistently refused to paint revolutionary scenes or subjects for propaganda. "Concerning
Courbet," Breton then writes, "it must be recognized that
everything happens as if he had deemed that the deep
faith he held in the amelioration of the world would find
means to be reflected in anything he decided to evoke
and would appear equally in the light he made fall on
the horizon or on a deer's belly." [78] An admirable phrase,
indicating to every intellectual, to every artist, his duty.
They are to follow, in perfect liberty, the proper necessities of genius, the evidence of sentiments and thoughts.

Can one, in fact, claim to emancipate men when one
has begun by betraying beauty and truth? This so simple and so essential question, it is surprising to note, has
in our time practically been posed only by André Breton. No matter how one conceives the relation between
social development and individual liberation, it still
seems that any revolutionary should try to make, at
least in his own mind, a synthesis of his desire for social
liberation and his concern for spiritual liberation. Can the
reasons that lead him to revolt politically against the
exploitation of man by man be separated from the indignation he feels at seeing certain men, men like himself, reduced to a lamentable state? And does this lamentable
state not include the error in which they are plunged and
the bad taste they rest in as well as the material poverty
and hunger that torment them? How can the conscious
revolutionary split up his desire of seeing man raised to a
higher dignity and, while objecting to people being
starved, accept that they should be lied to and made to

admire idiocies? How could he not agree with Breton
that the motto "more consciousness" is a unity and that
to "more social consciousness" we must add "but also
more psychological consciousness"? [79] The facts show,
however, that many of our contemporaries are insensi-
ble to these evidences or these duties. Calling themselves
partisans for the emancipation of men, they do not hesitate to lie to men. Must we believe then, as some do, that
they are really in the service of a new attempt at enslave-
ment? Must we be satisfied with the thought that the
political task seems so urgent to them that in cultural
matters they try merely to please the greatest numbers
and thus, aspiring to the lowest, in philosophy they adopt
the prejudices of common sense and in art the taste of
an amateur of the kitsch market? In any event the activity of these "intellectuals" (an expression they cherish)
could easily lead us to think that, contrary to the tenets
of Marxism, there is no connection between the march
of history and the development of culture. If this were
so, we would have to avow that the character of the
promise or annunciation proper to the most significant
works of art may in no wise be interpreted as a function
of a historical future. What then would the work of art—
for instance the beauty of the light that Courbet, according to Breton, made fall on the horizon or the deer's
belly—promise or announce? Either something "imaginary" without relation to any existence whatever or an
"other world" in the religious sense. But we know that
the surrealists refuse that despair, and also that faith.
Jean-Louis Bédouin (who for my part judges a bit
quickly that an attitude wanting to transform economic
realities and psychological realities at once is one "of the
clearest") [80] recalls in his study of Breton that the revolution must no longer be merely "against a capitalist
régime, but also against a Christian civilization." [81] From
this the surrealists seem reduced to the point (but who
today, who wants both to be sincere and not to go beyond pure knowledge, is not brought to this?) of cease-

lessly posing the question that crucifies Breton and with him, I think, all the artists and philosophers of this time: why is the political thought called leftist linked to the most reactionary and old-fashioned cultural thought? Why does the revolt by which man rises against the constraints weighing him down seem incompatible with the revolution?

III. Derealization

René Nelli once said to me of Breton, "He is right in a world that is wrong." I have often reflected on this appreciation. Although little drawn toward Hegelianism, I nevertheless ask myself if it is altogether permitted to go against the world and against the course of things. Is reality not richer than our thoughts? And is the norm of truth, which is that of our judgments, definable outside its relation to the World itself? In this connection we may ask if Breton has drawn the proper conclusions from the difficulties the contemporary world has brought him, from the opposition obvious everywhere between the eternal exigencies of man and his political desires, and if—projecting into the future the dimension proper to imagination—he has not sacrificed too much to the myth of history. Certainly, this myth is so constantly kept before us by recent philosophers that we may easily be tempted to take it as reality, supposing our spirit is "plunged" (as some put it) into history and into society. But it is precisely necessary not to confound the real with what our contemporaries may be pleased to think of it; an idea is not made false by being mishandled while being touted along the Boulevard St. Germain-des-Près. In fact, the idea of distinguishing two orders seems, more than any other, verified by reality and actuality. Never was spiritual history more separated from political history; never did reason feel, in the City, more solitary. From there, we may be allowed to think that there is nothing in common between the essential dissatisfaction that man feels in his natural condition, and the claims—just, no doubt, but interested and hence linked indissolubly to envy and resentment—which are at the base of revolutionary activity. Such claims are essentially technical and have meaning only in attempts at satisfaction. Pure revolt, on the contrary, is metaphysical, and if not canalized by hope in another world it can only lead to opposing our universe with a reality that is not and cannot be a world. But Breton tries to maintain, to all and against all, the unity of the idea of revolt and that of revolution. He is afraid that their dissociation will carry us back into dualism, which he rejects. Faithful to the essential demand of human consciousness, which is demand for the Other, he refuses to fall into a historicism that would be adoration of fact. But, unsatisfied by the negative character of pure metaphysics (which maintains the affirmation of the Other but leaves it undetermined) and refusing to make the Other into an "other world" in the sense that religions promise us, he is constrained to leave it to time, to leave for the future—in the form of an earthly state to come—the realization of his hope.

All sincere and well-directed minds, however, discover the same truth. Breton's exemplary fidelity to the authenticity of the human exigency should lead him, along the edge of his perhaps abused confidence in revolutionary realizations, to recover by his own ways the equivalent of the great metaphysical affirmations. Every metaphysics has appeared in some aspect as an enterprise toward disqualifying the reality of the World and its scientific and logical structure. The Cartesian theory of the creation of eternal verities asserts, beyond all knowable Nature, a Being totally independent not only of the physical laws that rule things but of the exigencies of our logic. Descartes can thus affirm that the World is a fable, a discourse deprived of ontological reality in the

plain sense of the word. Kant, opposing being to phenomenon, the unknowable thing-in-itself to the known
universe, situates scientific discourse on a level not that
of reality. Now the notion of surreality tends precisely,
with Breton, to remove authentic reality from the sway
of rational knowledge and logic. Breton, like the metaphysicians, perceives that the World is objective discourse and opposes discourse with existence, laws that
constrain—and are therefore metaphysically contingent
on the universe of science—with Being, the consciousness of which is tinged with infinity. He thus reveals,
like Descartes, that the faculty of negating, the basis of
all man's refusals, is not simply intellectual, a part of
judgment, and does not find its sole origin in the logical
contradictions of concepts or of known objects, but has
its source in this essential desire by which man is man,
desire which cannot be distinguished from freedom
(Descartes, in fact, did not distinguish between will and
liberty and, teaching that the soul is a unity, declared
that "all its appetites are volitions").[82]

Metaphysical and surrealist derealizations of the world
do present, however, an essential difference. Certainly,
Descartes is close to the surrealist dream and its entry
into waking life when he writes to Guez de Balzac,
"After sleep has sent my spirit rambling among boxwood,
through gardens and enchanted palaces, where I experience all the pleasures imagined in fables, insensibly I
mix my daytime reveries with those of the night, and
when I perceive that I am awake it is only so that my
contentment may grow more perfect and my senses participate."[83] But still Descartes' essential procedure consists, not in derealizing things, but in reconquering by
reason a real which he feels from the outset is not Being.
Hence the derealization of the knowable world and the
establishment of its foundation are the same thing:
Descartes' God is at once the Being who manifests that
nothing created is worthy the name of substance, and
the one who by his veracity nevertheless gives the basis

for a knowledge of Nature that is—in his system—certain. Kant's philosophy, which also distinguishes the scientifically knowable object from the thing-in-itself, likewise makes legitimate a science both rigorous and certain within its own order. Thus, the solution for Descartes and Kant lies in dualism. But Breton, rejecting dualism, cannot go outside the world to find the nonlogical Being to which he aspires. He must discover it in this very world, which forbids him to preserve the solidity and structure of the knowable world. It is from within the knowable and the given that he must bring forth the prodigies of surreality. The difficulty that the classic metaphysicians resolved by setting up two levels here becomes a conflict within the order, now unique and as if horizontal, of the World, and we can see how the Hegelian theme of opposites and their dialectic resolution tempted surrealism to this extent. Nevertheless Breton is farther from Hegel than from Descartes. Hegel's solution is notional and rational synthesis. Breton's operates on the level of existence that hope for real life reveals to us directly as irreducible to any conceptual form—existence that by this fact is far closer to the cogito and Being of Descartes than to the Hegelian synthesis.

Derealization is always, with the surrealists, the fruit of an experience and uses rational discourse only to negate it, taking the opposite of its constitutive laws. It never results from an order of reasons. It illuminates, completely apart from logic, the essential tension that coincides with becoming conscious of the whole man, man as he is. Although its tone is quite different and more aesthetic than ethical or religious, the surrealist experience is somewhat analogous to that of Kierkegaard. He discovers subjectivity by his revolt against the System, refusing to be one of its parts, one of its moments. Now the Hegelian system was disgraced by seeing in political man (and at a certain moment in Napoleon) the philosopher himself. At the time surrealism was born, human discourse was likewise disgraced by a ridiculous justification of the war, an abject complaisance for the values to which—in spite of a drama and sufferings judged convenient to forget—one comfortably returned. Armchair moralists, never quitting their armchairs, in the name of propriety and decorum and proper manners, banned love and life to those coming back from death. Then, after the Dada interlude—the fruit of a negation expressing hardly more than the disillusioned irony of an initial fatigue that showed decline from 1921—burst the surrealist revolt. The faculty of negating was expressed with unprecedented violence. They literally would not listen to anything. Man established his claims on the level of immediacy, without concern for the necessities of logic. They came to the very source of desire and set it up as supreme norm. True, it was again a matter of enlarging the consciousness; it was an attempt—in the face of man's technical powers whose extent and misguidedness the war revealed—to raise the consciousness of ends to a level with the consciousness of means. But this could not take place without a vehement protest against the necessities to which, precisely, the consciousness of means had enslaved man. The surrealist rejection and fury were addressed, in an elective manner, to the justification of means, to the sadly famous "we must go through that." And thus, I think, surrealism was brought to rise up against the rational logos, against the immanent structure of things, to pass from the rejection of human discourse to the rejection of the discourse which constitutes the World of perception and of science. Surrealism perceives moreover, recovering the profound sense of the Cartesian *Mundus est fabula,* that these discourses are at bottom only a single discourse: "Does not the mediocrity of our universe," Breton asks himself in fact, "depend essentially on our power of enunciation?" [84] And again: "What keeps me from scrambling the word order, thus attacking the completely seeming existence of things?" [85] We

see here why Breton could never consent to make action
into a properly political conception, why each time that
difficulties made him choose between practical efficacy
and poetry he chose poetry. It was above all to evade
these "justifications," of which the war literature had
furnished such degrading examples and which fill re-
pressive education, and those recipes or rules of procedure acquired in any apprenticeship. Rimbaud had
already said, "I have a horror of all trades. Masters and
workers, all peasants, ignoble. The hand with the pen is
worth the hand on the plough—What a century of
hands!—I shall never have my hand." [86] When surrealism writes, "War against work," [87] it is following Rimbaud.

Thus, desire, subordinated by technology to the measure and to the laws of its effective powers, returns to its
childlike and primal project of derealization. Those who
wish to see satanism in the surrealist revolt will now say
that having rebelled against God the Father, whose image is always linked to that of the actual father who gives
the child orders contrary to the child's desires, surrealism
rebels against the Word as Malebranche understood it,
that is, against the very order which is that of things.
The identity in the two cases of the word "order" is
rich in significance and Kant has well shown how, even
though hypothetical (if you want this, do that), the
technical imperative is none the less an imperative for
volition. In fact, reason, although in a sense it is interior
to man, although it constitutes for man a power for
emancipation and criticism in regard to any authority
arbitrarily imposed on him, and although in its very
technique it appears as an instrument in the service of
his needs, remains foreign to man to the extent that man,
in search of unity, coincides with his desire. Reason is
confounded with the laws of things imposed on us to
which we must submit. It assumes the face of exteriority,
and this is why Descartes said that all rational comprehension is passion.[88] Thus, reason becomes what irritates

our impatience. It is by essence detour and presupposes the proper conduct for detours. If I want to enter a room the door of which opens toward me, I must, in order to open the door, first make a step backward and thus— to satisfy my desire—go opposite to my desire. The pure activity of desire in this case would be to get angry and try to break the door down by hurling myself against it. One cannot doubt that surrealism has sometimes chosen, against the detour of reason, the violence of anger, that is, the authenticity of pure desire. Again, one must not suppose that it has chosen the absurd. It wants only not to let human desire be lost and forgotten in the meanderings of a patience that, as seen every day, ends by depriving action of its aim, deflecting wonder into technique and the sacred into politics. "Who knows," asks Breton on the contrary, "but what I might contribute in that way toward ruining those concrete trophies, so detestable, toward throwing a greater discredit over those beings and those things of 'reason'? There would be machines cunningly put together which would remain without employment. One could draw up elaborate plans for immense cities that, no matter our number, we would feel forever incapable of founding, but which would at least include present and future capitals. Absurd and quite perfected robots, which would do nothing like anyone else, would be put in charge of giving us a correct idea of action." [89] Breton's hatred of machines is already expressed in *Poisson soluble:* "We shall, at great expense, set at the bottom of the water machines that have ceased to serve, and also a few others that began to serve, and it is a pleasure to see the mud voluptuously paralysing what functioned so well. We are the creators of wrecks ... We take our post of aquatic command of these balloons, of these nasty vessels constructed on the principle of the lever, winch, and inclined plane. We run hither and yon to make certain everything is lost." [90]

"Everything the heart desires can be reduced to the figure of water," Claudel said. And Gaston Bachelard,

who cites the phrase, remarks that Claudel dreams of
finding in the bosom of the Earth "a veritable essential
water, a water substantially religious." "This subterranean lake dreamt by the visionary poet will give thus a subterranean sky." [91] Undoubtedly, with Breton the world of
water is also in many respects the object of a fundamental
hope. Not that water is linked here (as, according to
Bachelard, is often the case) with purification. It is
linked rather with the fluidity of desire and opposes the
world of solid matter, the objects of which may be constructed into machines, with a world akin to our childhood, where the constraining laws of reason have no
sway. This water is manifested ceaselessly and under a
myriad different forms in the most spontaneous writings
of Breton. The first text of *Poisson soluble* [92] tells us of a
magic fountain, seabirds, the dew of evening, sweat of
stars, a fish-gondola, river of flowers, vessels going to bed
in the silver tempest, the echo of rain and of tears,
cloud-edge and island beach, water beasts, a woman ad-
miring her feet in a puddle of winter water, a waterfall
falling between my life's theater and me, seas where one
dives to bring up the branch of blood coral. And Breton
writes significantly, "At the moment she sleeps, facing
the infinite of my loves, before this mirror tarnished by
terrestrial breathing. It is in sleep that she really belongs
to me." Thus, in order to be possessed by desire, the
world must be deprived of the hardness of its physical
structure, the woman of the hardness of her conscious
structure; the dream derealizes the world, sleep takes
the woman from the empire of reason which, awake,
gives to her conduct a calculated coherence and by this
fact excludes the lover and his curbless demands.

Certainly, no one has gone as far as Dali in the path
of this derealizing and possessive desire. Like Breton,
Dali perceives the relationship between water and the
fluidity of the object assimilated by desire. Extolling
"art nouveau" in 1900 architecture, he saw in it "hard
undulations of sculptured water," the "sculpture of re-

flections of twilight clouds in water, rendered possible by recourse to an immense and senseless mosaic, multi-colored and gleaming, pointillist iridescences from which emerge forms of water spilled, forms of water spilling, forms of water stagnant, forms of mirroring water, forms of water curled by the wind," etc. From there Dali attempts in the plastic arts to substitute for an emotion whose basis would still be to search into the laws proper to the sense of vision, and thus in a way into reason, a gustatory emotion linked to what is most primitive in human desire, most destructive of its object, most irrational—hunger. Dali speaks to us of the "edible" beauty of art nouveau architecture. "The soft base of this column seems to say to us: Eat me," he writes. He notes among the general characteristics of the phenomenon the "profound depreciation of intellectual systems," "total aesthetic unconsciousness," "hatred of reality," "majestic blossoming of unconscious erotic-irrational tendencies," and, after having dreamt of grottoes one would penetrate "by tender doors of calves' liver," concludes: "Beauty will be edible or will not be at all." [93] We may explain by this aesthetics the viscous and irrational character of the famous soft structures of Dali, for example those watches that seem to spread out and flow in the manner of overripe cheeses.[94] It is clear that in this, according to the law of desire-hunger that can possess only in destroying what it desires, the object is led to deny itself the better to offer itself to us: the soft watch, in coming to seem like a Camembert, negates its essence of watch, since a soft object cannot hold clockworks. The soft object is the negation of any machine and, by that, of any process in physics.

Dali is, however, the only one strictly to have linked derealization with the digestive and, as he says, "cannibal" human desire. Certainly, with all the surrealists derealization, like revolt, is only a means. It is a matter of man, the whole man, formed of appetite as well as reason, affirming his unity and the totality of his rights. But

desire, as the surrealists understand it, is often less possessive than curious and ecstatic; the world of marvels
to which poetry must conduct us is not reducible to the
isle of syrup and nougat dear to good gluttonous children. It promises more revelatory ecstasies. Hence surrealism must, in order to derealize the world of everyday
action, include techniques other than fluidification. These
techniques most often have recourse to surprise and be-
wilderment; they lead the object to reject its proper
sense by deceiving our habitual expectation. The guitar
with epaulettes or the ultra-home-furnishing (a stool
supported by feminine legs) of Kurt Seligmann and the
iron bristling with spikes by Man Ray [95] are first of all
objects deflected from their sense, rendered inappropri-
ate to their technical end in order to bring to light that
end without end that according to Kant is proper to
beauty. Breton here reminds us of the example of Marcel
Duchamp "going in quest of friends to show them a cage
that looked birdless but was half filled with sugar cubes,
asking them to lift the cage. They were astonished to find
it so heavy, what they had taken for sugar cubes being
actually small pieces of marble that Duchamp, at great
expense, had had cut to those dimensions." [96] For my
own part, I am always pleased to recognize in this trick
an example provoked by that disappointment before the
real which I am convinced is at the origin of any metaphysical approach. And we know how sensitive Breton is
to the beauty of Berkeley's philosophy, which in denying
the existence of matter is a philosophy of derealization.[97]
But while the metaphysician suffers the deception of
what Breton calls the "not much of reality" and tries to
establish on solid bases the world that he feels escaping
him, the surrealist attempts voluntarily to provoke the
given into collapsing. He tends to produce a "fundamental crisis of the object," [98] to "bewilder sensation," [99] and
this task of disintegration is the first he proposes for
what he names poetry. "Look," Breton says, "how highly
poetry regards the possible and how it loves the unlikely.

What is, what might be, how insufficient that seems to
it! Nature, poetry denies your sway; things, what cares
poetry for your properties? It knows no respite till it has
held out over the entire universe its negativistic hand." [100]
 The study of all the procedures by which surrealist
poetry tends to derealize the world by the rupture of
logical relations discoverable among its objects and even
inside its objects (an object is, in effect, only a bundle
of qualities linked by constant relations, veritable laws)
would easily persuade us that for the surrealists we
cannot recover the pristine and childlike consciousness,
where the original rapport between spirit and thing is
manifested, if we have not first undertaken to destroy the
results of that rational and verbal solidification of our
experience which in most men takes the place of reality.
Language, where reason is crystalized, is thus going to
be put through a hard ordeal and all those will be ap-
plauded who, before surrealism, found in its phrases a
paralogical sense, such as Jean-Pierre Brisset claiming
that "all ideas pronounced with similar sounds...re-
fer...at their base to a single object," and concluding
(if one can speak here of conclusions) from the words
"the teeth, the mouth" ("les dents, la bouche") that the
teeth plug up the entrance of the mouth ("les dents la
bouchent"), that the teeth are the aid or support of the
mouth ("l'aide en la bouche"), etc.[101] Picabia, obviously
conscious in a different way of the scope of his discoveries, is praised for having "been the first to comprehend
that all combinations of words without exception are
legitimate and that their poetic quality is the greater the
more they appear to be gratuitous or irritating at first
sight." [102] Madness itself is called in to help. Having
recalled Kraepelin's definition of paranoid states, states
responding "to the insidious development, contingent on
internal causes and by a continuous evolution, of a system of delirium that is durable and unshakable and
which is established with complete conservation of clarity and order in thought, volition and action," Breton

declares that "artists present a certain number of tendencies in common with paranoiacs." "There is no
doubt," he adds, "it is to the extent the artist is capable
of reproducing and objectifying by painting or any other
means the exterior objects to whose restraints he sadly
submits that he escapes to a great extent from the tyranny of those objects and avoids being felled by psychosis proper." Psychosis, for all that, does not cease to
tempt surrealism, which adopts the paranoid-critical
activity championed by Dali—"spontaneous method of
irrational knowledge based on interpretative critical association of the phenomena of madness." [103] And we are
aware of the texts of *L'Immaculée conception* titled "The
Possessions," [104] in which Breton and Eluard simulate
feeble-mindedness, acute mania, paresis, *délire d'inter-
prétation,* and dementia praecox. "We declare ourselves,"
the authors write, "particularly pleased with this new
exercise of our thought. We have here realized in ourselves resources up till now unsuspected." [105]

And, of course, the spirit is not invited to founder in
madness but on the contrary to "submit voluntarily to
the basic mad ideas without his having a durable trouble." [106] Surrealism is faithful to the "long, immense and
reasoned derangement of all the senses" that Rimbaud
advocated in his letter of May 15, 1871. Not satisfied with
overturning verbal structures, it inverts and modifies
the basic attitude of consciousness, gives the pleasure
principle entire authority over the reality principle, exalts the liberty vision has to see what it wants to, the
freedom consciousness has of conferring on objects the
sense it chooses. Breton relates how, at the psychiatric
center of the Second Army at Saint-Dizier, he knew a
patient who maintained that the war "was only a sham.
The blank shells could do no harm, the men apparently
wounded were all done with makeup." [107] The argument
of this patient and "the impossibility of making him give
it up" made a "strong impression" on Breton. "It is certain," Breton adds, "that for me there is a certain temp-

tation in that." And how, in fact, not be tempted by the powers of an imagination we should call, neither creative nor reproductive, but negative or derealizing, if such a faculty allowed a single man to deny all the horror of World War I and see nothing in it but a gigantic spectacle, a sumptuous hoax. Thus, desire and human instinct, when the path of political transformation of the real is seen to be deceptive, invent or discover a world in which they can be satisfied. This world is perhaps that of sadism, if it is true that for many the prestige of the sadistic act is not in realization but in imagination. It is assuredly that of dream, whose Universe surrealism has always exalted for being able to depreciate and overturn our universe. It is, in the waking state, that of the marvelous, castles and phantoms for evocation of which Breton and Julien Gracq show such inclination. The note to the reader before *Au château d'Argol* brings up with favor "the always striking repertory of dilapidated castles, sounds, lights, spectres in the night, and dreams." [108] And Breton at the beginning of *Nadja* extends derealization from the realm of objects to that of the ego itself. Asking himself, "Who am I?" he comes via the old saying to ask whom he "haunts," and hence to appear in "the role of a phantom." [109] The crisis of object thus becomes crisis of subject and of the real in general.

   In this universal derealization there is no doubt but what humor, and particularly what the surrealists call black humor, plays a special role. Without wishing to propose a definition of humor (which Breton says is impossible) and without stopping to comment on the psychological interpretation of Freud, who sees first of all the ego's refusal "to be hurt by the arrows of reality or to be compelled to suffer," [110] I would venture to point out how humor stamps all reality with the character of nonexistence. Breton cites Pierre Piobb, "Laughter . . . is at the edge of nothingness, deposits nothingness with us as security," [111] and the *Dictionnaire abrégé du*

surréalisme recalls the definition of humor by Jacques
Vaché, "I believe it is a sensation—I almost said a
sense—also—of the theatrical (and joyless) futility of
everything." [112] No doubt all aesthetic perception presupposes a first derealization, a rupture with the attitude
whereby we take immediate possession of the real: I
can judge a painted landscape only if I know first of all
that the canvas which represents it is not a window open
to the countryside, or a play only by thinking that the
action I witness is not real (otherwise I would go up on
the stage like the naive peasant to put a stop to the
murders and warn the victims of plots against them).
This aesthetic derealization, by which the spirit corrects
itself, is all that keeps artistic perception from being
madness. Still, the perception of art allows a rather direct
adhesion to the subject treated, noticeable for instance
in our desire for a novel to end well or, with paintings,
in our reference to the thing represented. But reading a
text of black humor demands a second derealization,
like a negation to the second degree, a negation of negation. Jules Vuillemin told me once of the indignation of
a simple man reading, but obviously incapable of taking
the suitable attitude toward, the "Mauvais vitrier" of
Baudelaire (a text in which Baudelaire tells how he
tricked a glazier into coming up, sent him back down
with the pretext that he had no panes of a color to make
one "see life beautifully," then as the man passed below,
broke all of his glass by dropping a flower pot).[113] Likewise, if we looked with ordinary perspective, the proposal of Swift to use the children of the poor as meat for
rich men's tables [114] or Allais' telling how he had a "good
laugh" over a neighbor woman's death that he himself
had provoked [115] would be simply intolerable. Black humor demands quite a special application of what might
be called our negative apprehension. It presupposes our
power to take everything upside down, or at least wrong
side up. Is it necessary to point out that thus characterized it finds its chosen land in the admirable and contin-

ually misunderstood work of Alfred Jarry, a work to which only the surrealists rendered full justice?

But derealization is not an end in itself or a means of evasion. As such, it suffices neither to transform the world nor to change life. Thanks to the properly undefinable grasp on the real to which it conducts us by various ways, it at least permits a consciousness that both the rational categories and the necessities of practical choice forbade. All our tendencies (including, naturally, our tendencies toward cruelty) are here revealed in all their contradiction. And yet, as Gracq remarks, it is not a question of "fusing the elements that howl to be reconciled into a sort of eclecticism." [116] Rather it is necessary to discover the essential ambivalence, which does not exclude unity, of the affective consciousness. It is necessary to recognize true man, his spirit with its numberless powers, his infinite desires; only by him can one judge any task undertaken toward transforming the universe or changing existence. This is why the film *L'Age d'or* is head and shoulders above the painful simplemindedness of propaganda films which attempt to lead the spectator to adhere to a revolutionary idea in the very name of the ethics and spiritual state that was created by the society they pretend to want to destroy, and which illustrate minutely, like the novels of the *Veillées des chaumières*, the classic and puerile distinction between the good and the bad, according the good all virtues and to the bad nothing but pure meanness. In surrealism, on the contrary, man is revealed in his concrete mystery; it appears that we will judge every proposition from now on according to pristine and fundamental consciousness, consciousness existing before any acquisition or any elaboration, consciousness from which representation of the real and of the imaginary are derived, consciousness whose approach suffices to throw our considered projects into the most profound disquiet. The search in this is always for unity, reconciliation of man with the real and with himself: after praising Picasso for his "experiments in disintegration," Breton tries to define "that point at which artistic creation, the aim of which is to affirm the hostility that can animate the being's desire with respect to the external world, succeeds in fact in rendering the exterior object adequate to this desire and thus in reconciling the world itself, to a certain extent, with being." [117] But the reconciliation of man with the real and with himself is not sought for in a supreme synthesis which will illuminate the end of time, after having put into play all rational mediations. It is not sought for in labor, supposedly realizing the supreme unification of man and Nature in recovering a sense and, as it were, a purposiveness that only social alienation had made it lose. The spirit surpasses reason and, even in a classless society, labor would presuppose effort, limitation to a specialized task, submission to the laws of technique; it lacks in any case the element of ravishment and of pleasure which the untricked consciousness of man asks. Any methodical project, any effort, any reason, any structure will thus for the surrealists rejoin the object and be inscribed in the exteriority of a world that man does not feel to his measure. From then, the eminent reality of man suffices to derealize this world itself, in its impatient expectation of that surreality which alone could fulfill a desire that is already revealed in its totality by the insatiable marvelings of our childhood. The basis of the surrealist procedure is not Hegelian reason or Marxist labor; it is liberty.

Chapter Three

Expectation and the Interpretation of Signs

1. Love

Derealization of the everyday world was always, for the surrealists, in the positive hope of possession and discovery. Surrealism is not flight into the unreal or into dream, but an attempt to penetrate into what has more reality than the logical and objective universe. It is easy thus to connect its animating need with expectation for a beyond, to confound the surrealist consciousness with the religious consciousness; both are in search of Being and make much of adoration. But, unlike the religious beyond, the surrealist beyond cannot be placed outside this world or past our lifetime. It is, paradoxically, an immanent beyond, inside the very beings whose appearance we experience, whose presence we perceive. One can discover its manifestation only in states that any man can feel in this world and where the object, seeming to surpass itself, is revealed at once as common and quasi-holy, natural and overwhelming. Breton declares that "surprise," which according to him "must be sought for itself alone, unconditionally," "exists only in the intricate mingling in a single object of the natural and the supernatural." [1] This is why love (read passion-love) immediately takes first place in surrealist preoccupation. In it are found once more all the prodigies of the Universe, all the powers of consciousness, all the agitation of feeling. It effects the supreme synthesis of subjective and objective and restores to us the ravishment that surrealist sunderings seemed to make impossible. It is from love that the surrealists expect the great revelation and their moral concern often seems no more than taking care to be worthy of it. As Char writes, "In the irreconcilable domain of surreality, the privileged man" can only be prey "to his devouring life-purpose: love." [2]

But love cannot be an end in itself, since in its deepest intention it is love for something that one loves. Already in the *Symposium* Socrates refutes in this way Agathon's rhetorical panegyric on love; love, he says, is love of something other than itself, it tends toward what it does not have. So all narcissistic forms of love are outlawed; real love is love of exteriority. Loving is going outside oneself, not loving one's loving self. Surrealism does not escape this logic. It often sees in love self-forgetfulness. "She loves, she loves to forget herself," Eluard writes.[3] He glorifies the loved being, that is, woman, who thus takes, in the surrealist scale of values, the place of God.[4] The texts where this ecstatic adoration is expressed are numberless. Here is Aragon: "Sweet lady of wind, reaper of light, you whose pure hair by a route streaked with comets is smuggled to my eyes..."[5] "Woman, you take even so the place of all form. Hardly had that abandon slipped my mind and even the black unconcern that you love, when here you are again and everything dies at your footfall. At your footfall on the sky a shadow envelops me. At your footfall toward night I lose distractedly all memory of the day. Charming substitute, you are the abstract of a marvelous world, of the natural world, and it is you reborn when I close my eyes. You are the wall and its chink. You are horizon and presence. The ladder and the steel rungs. Total eclipse. Light. Miracle: and can we think of anything but miracle when the miracle is here in a robe of night? So the universe for me little by little fades, dissolves, while from its depths an adorable phantom arises, a tall woman ascends, at last fully outlined, who appears everywhere without anything to separate me from her in the most solid aspect of an ending world.... Mountains, you will never be anything but the distance of this woman.... Here I am no longer but a drop of rain on her skin, or dew.... Pass over, pass over my palms, water like tears, boundless woman in whom I am completely bathed. Pass over my sky, my silence, my veils." [6] There is no need to compare such pages with the most noted texts of Christian mysticism; they are an exact transposition and at the same time the opposite, since here it is the woman who rises at the fall of the abandoned world, takes her place, then finds the world again in order to contain it and to contain me, thus becoming that eminent reality in which we "move, and have our being." The mystique of obedience and of submission is also close to that of participation and of engulfment. "Who is there? who calls me? Dearest. I do not rebel, I come running. Here are my lips. Then hides. And then afterward. I naturally not difficult. Damned, damned. That I collapse, beat me, melt me. I am your creature, your victory, better yet my own defeat." [7] With Eluard, the loved woman likewise appears as negator of the Universe.

> *Her dreams in broad daylight*
> *Make suns evaporate* [8]

Then, as what occupies him commands him and animates him:

> *I hear your voice vibrate in all the world's noises* [9]
> *...And days and nights ruled by your eyelids* [10]

Finally, as what creates him and creates me:

> *...Aureole of time, nocturnal and certain cradle,*
> *And if I know no longer all I have lived through,*
> *It is because your eyes have not always beheld me.*

> *... As the day is upheld by innocence*
> *The whole world hangs from your pure eyes*
> *And all my blood flows in their glances.*[11]

For Breton woman is often last in a similar mystic procession; coming after a suite of marvelous omens that announce her, she takes the place of the absolute: "You replace the forms that were most familiar to me, as well as many figures of my presentiment. . . .

"All I know is that that replacement stops with you, because you are not replaceable by anything, and for me it was from all eternity that with you the succession of terrible or charming enigmas had to end.

"You are not an enigma for me.

"I say that you turn me forever from the enigma.

"Since you exist, as you only know how to exist. . . ."[12]

But we cannot hide the fact that such a conception of love, though it inspires admirable lyric texts, offers philosophically the gravest difficulties. Even without adopting unreservedly the religious criticisms of the surrealist conception of love, we must allow with them that it is uncomfortable to replace, in human aspirations, Being, or the Absolute, by woman. In effect, either the demand of desire will be directed toward woman in general and will from then on, in all the tireless quest of libertinage, embrace only an abstraction and an idea, or else passion-love will persuade us that all value resides in the single loved woman (but in this case our consciousness will always preserve enough lucidity to denounce the error of a belief so contrary to reason and introduce again, into the experience of love, sorrow and the feeling of separation). Actually, surrealism has always hesitated between elective love and love of the Feminine.

At the front of an anthology of poems Eluard symptomatically places the passage from the *Mémoires d'outre-tombe* in which Chateaubriand confesses that in his search for a love that would be "supreme felicity" he composed one woman from all the women he had seen:

"She had the figure, hair, and smile of the foreign woman who had pressed me to her breast; I gave her the eyes of a certain girl from the village, the freshness of another. The portraits of great ladies from the age of Francis I, of Henri IV, and of Louis XIV that adorned the salon furnished me with other features and I had even stolen graces from paintings of the Virgin hung in churches." [13] In a different but analogous experience, Eluard discovers through various encounters a unique femininity:

> And it is always the same avowal, the same youth, the same pure eyes, the same unspoiled movement of her arms about my neck, the same caress, the same revelation.
>
> But it is never the same woman.
>
> The cards have stated that I will meet her in this life, but will not recognize her.[14]

Still, if the loved woman is a chimera born from my imagination or an abstract presence incapable of being incarnated altogether or being recognized in a single body, must we not admit that love—the idea of which Breton declares is "alone sufficient to reconcile any man ... with the idea of life" [15]—promises more than it delivers? It does not produce its object; we are once more reduced to waiting, and the hope for love that animated surrealism's first steps becomes a hope for hope. We understand the concern that in 1929 provoked the *Enquête sur l'amour,* whose principal question was precisely, "What sort of hope do you put in love?" [16] And we must recognize that most of the answers given by the surrealists to this question have only a poetic interest and turn logically in a circle.[17] How can this circle be broken without declaring that the loved woman is not only she that resembles the Lovable, but that the Lovable is she? If we refuse to subscribe to such a paradoxical affirmation, in other words if we do not submit entirely to passionate blindness, if we do not on the other hand wish to fall into a short-sighted naturalism content to

see in erotic excitement an objectless illusion sprung
from powerful impulses but totally devoid of light, we
must simply consider love as sign of a reality surpassing
what, properly speaking, experience presents to us: an
individual being clearly worth less than hundreds of
others. Here we are back to Plato, for whom the reflective deepening in the expectation of love always
leads us to the discovery of some impersonal value and,
finally, to the world of Ideas, our souls' native land,
which is not this present world. In this sense, Plato holds
libertinage, not of course sensual but filled in each of its
experiences with erotic emotion, as closer to the essence
of love than a love exclusive and faithful. And in effect
libertinage keeps us from confounding the beauty that
moves us with one or another of the individual beings
who, momentarily, manifest it. For my part, I have never
managed to escape this logic: If beauty is capable of
moving us this way in different faces, is it not distinct
from its incarnations, and superior to them? And should
we not admit then that in the midst of love some yonder
signals us?

Such, however, is not Breton's opinion. Careful to avoid
all transcendence, he subordinates love to the individual
being that constitutes its present object, and consequently
favors a love elective and unique. "In love," he says,
"I have opted for the passionate and exclusive kind."
And remembering how this conception has clashed with
"that of sceptics or even more or less declared libertines,"
he remarks that most of the quarrels arising within
surrealism have been "overdetermined" by an "irreducible
disagreement on this point." [18] Such a position leads
Breton to claim that love cannot decline or disappear:
"There is no more formidable sophism than that which
consists in presenting the accomplishment of the sexual
act as necessarily accompanied by a fall in amorous
potential between two beings, a fall whose return would
progressively trail off toward insufficiency. Thus, love
would be exposed to its ruin in proportion as it pursued

its very realization.... The being, here, would be called upon to lose little by little its elective character for another, it would be against its will reduced to essence.... Nothing is more callous, more distressing than this conception." [19] Distressing perhaps, but how avoid it? Personally, we see only one way, that being to return to a Christian conception, according to which love is addressed to the very substance of the loved being and, to speak more clearly, to her person. But to condemn libertinage we must cease to place at the root of love excitement in the presence of beauty and passionate upheaval. Does Breton consent to this? No, his philosophy is not personalistic, his love is a thousand leagues from the Christian "caritas," sensual upheaval before the beautiful retains its eminence for him. Can a radical distinction be established from this, as Breton would like, between elective love and libertine love? Is it not advisable rather to distinguish within libertinism itself the vain search for physical joys or the pleasure of conquest and domination, sensations hardly rising above the level of gluttony or a sordid will to power, and authentic ravishment, adoration that makes one swoon, feelings that cannot be separated from what is deepest in love and that manifest its essence? Breton avows that he was "for a long time hard put to argue validly" against the libertines in defense of his conception of love.[20] And in fact the texts of *L'amour fou* devoted to this problem, whether they probe into the idea of the decline of love from social and moral causes,[21] or invoke the authority of Engels to the effect that "individual sexual love," born from monogamy, is "the greatest moral progress man has accomplished in modern times," [22] are not very convincing. They seem to us to refer less to the experience of love than to a certain idea of love, which we may legitimately fear is only a prejudice. In any case, when Breton declares that love such as he conceives it "must conquer," [23] he goes no further than to formulate a wish. "What I have loved," he says again, "whether I have kept it or not, I shall always love it."[24] It seems difficult to grant this affirmation any sense beyond that of a decision; it expresses in any case no truth, since Breton himself declares he has loved, successively and with passion, several women.

The plurality of women loved, "these over the years, those some day,"[25] is evoked at the beginning of *L'amour fou*. They appear seated opposite several personages "dressed in black" representing Breton loving them. Keeping to the logic of this first image, we would again find that radical discontinuity that in other texts Breton wanted to establish beween the moments of his life, and the problem of the rapport between successive loves of a single lover would not be posed. But the narrative takes a different turn. "Enter one man . . . he recognizes them: one after the other? all at once?" This simple question again introduces, at least as hypothesis, the idea of an essence common to all the loves taken successively. Breton, however, again rejects the idea, declaring that the lover will discover finally "in all these women's faces only one face: the last face loved."[26] Once more we are back with the unique love; the women loved earlier would be for the lover only the annunciation and promise of the woman loved now. Only this one would be truly loved, the others having been loved only by illusion and, as it were, by their relation to her. But Breton has some trouble holding on to this conception, more moving than true. According to him the lover, discovering in all the faces of the woman he has loved "only one face, the last face loved," recognizes likewise in all the male faces opposite "only himself." Now in this the text lacks coherence; in order for the parallelism to be maintained, Breton would have to reduce all the masculine persons that he evokes, not to the lover "himself," but to the lover at that moment, the last lover. For it is one thing to affirm the identity of my self across successive loves and quite another to suppose that all these loves have reality and finality only in the last among them.

In the latter case, we maintain that a single being was really loved and a single one really loving. In the former we recognize that the lover was always the same through various loves; we accept thus some transcendence of the self in relation to its successive loves. And the correlative of this unique lover can no longer be the last woman loved, but a type present in all the loved women. It seems in this sense significant to note Breton, without renouncing his idea of the last face loved, nevertheless writing, "The loved being would be then the one in whom were comprised a certain number of particular qualities held to be more attractive than others and appreciated separately, successively, in the beings loved earlier to some degree. Note that this proposition corroborates, in dogmatic form, the popular notion of such and such an individual's type of woman or man." [27] The notions of quality and of type bring us back, however, and this time without possibility of return, to a Platonic conception in which no concrete and finite being can take the place of the Lovable or become the unique goal of Love. Thus, we always return to our problem: if the loved woman is not the unique and sufficient object of love, what reality does her image signify? What does she reflect for us? What is it that love waits for? What sort of hope must we put in love?

The *Symposium* of Plato, which presents, I believe, all the possible hypotheses concerning the nature of a love supposed to awaken at sight of a physical form (in other words of any love other than the Christian "caritas"), contains a reply to these questions deliberately oriented toward unity and finiteness: the reply of Aristophanes. (This is not, of course, Plato's answer.) Aristophanes declares that once upon a time men were each made of two of the human beings of the sort we know. They had four hands, four legs, two faces. These beings were very strong and immensely proud; they decided to attack the gods. Zeus, to counteract their revolt and weaken them, cut them in two. Present man is thus only half a being, and such is the primal source of love. Each searches for what he was separated from, the half he lost, and in the embraces of love seeks to recover the unity he once knew. The logic of these images had to lead Breton, one of whose major tendencies also points toward the valorization of the single human and thus of finiteness, to recover the myth. His aspiration to "possess truth in one soul and one body" [28] . . . "suffices to unroll before it the allegorical field where every human being has been thrown into life searching for a being of the opposite sex and one in particular to which he is in all respects matched, to the point that one without the other seems like a product of dissociation, the dislocation of a single block of light." [29] Thus, the theme of recognition-love is justified. "Before knowing you," Breton writes, "—come now, those words are nonsense. You know perfectly well the first time I saw you I recognized you without the slightest hesitation." [30] Eluard's line, "We are reunited beyond the past," [31] expresses the same certitude. In this sense we must say that what announces love is still a personal and fundamental verity—my irreplaceable destiny. Nelli has illuminated this aspect of surrealist love. "If the surrealists," he writes, "valorize woman and love, it is only in the name of the unconscious destiny that is searching for itself at once in lover and loved, and in order to prove that one can love only a being capable of incarnating or symbolizing our earthly fate or, at the very least, of passing through it." [32] "To want to love," Nelli says further, "is thus henceforward to fall for a determinism that, instead of passing by over our heads, goes inside us, puts us in the world, makes us attend our own apparition." [33] But Nelli perceives that surrealist love is something other still, forgetfulness of our limitations, "negation of the individual to the profit of an objective world whose reverse it is." [34] To my mind there is an inspiration there not quite reconcilable logically with the one preceding: the woman, unique and sufficient, object of a love that reveals only her and me, the woman of whom Eluard could write:

> *We played in the sun in the rain in the sea*
> *At having only one glance one sky one sea*
> *Ours* [35]

is succeeded by the woman signifying something other than her and me, incarnating a universal value, containing in a kind of eternity the secret of the World. Such is the woman "who has always subjugated the poets because time has no hold on her," [36] the woman with the "transcendental vocation" to whom we may turn for "earthly salvation," [37] the woman who permits Breton to write: "The great malediction is lifted, in human love resides all power for the regeneration of the world," [38] lastly the woman-key in whom Breton perceives "the very image of the secret, of one of the great secrets of nature." [39] It is clear that here woman announces the order of impersonal truth or, in any case, something that surpasses her own reality and belongs outside her. How then pretend further that love "which consents . . . to recognize its object only in a single being" realizes "in the highest degree the fusion of existence and essence"? [40] Quite the contrary, in this love the existential contingency is surpassed by essence, essence of beauty and of truth expressed by the being one loves. We will not get around Platonism.

The surrealist conception is thus perfectly clear in that it refuses the ridiculous explanation of human love by the sexual instinct, in that it affirms that love, far from a vain or mistaken exaltation in the service of the species' interest, as biological amateurs say, possesses a sense, carries a valuable revelation, expresses what Breton, renouncing the materialist vocabulary, calls in *Arcane 17* "the spiritual life." [41] But it remains ambiguous as soon as the question arises of what, precisely, love signifies. Love announces, but what does it announce?

Is it my own destiny, is it the future of history, as we might sometimes think seeing Breton ask that the "power" be put back into women's hands,[42] is it the eternity the woman-child seems the sign of,[43] is it the very secret of the World? We can only take up again *Nadja's* anxious questioning: "Who goes there? Who goes there? Is it you Nadja? Is it true that the beyond, all the beyond, is in this life? I do not understand you. Who goes there? Is it I alone? Is it myself?" [44] Thus, surrealism, though it describes the human experience of love with an exactitude and depth perhaps heretofore unknown, does not succeed in elucidating that experience. Eluard writes:

You are water turned back from its abysses
You are earth that takes root
And on which all things are established.

. . . .

You sacrifice time
To the eternal youth of the exact flame
Which veils nature while reproducing her.

Woman you bring into the world a body always like
Yours

You are resemblance.[45]

What does this poem signify? What does the loved woman resemble? Is she the source of the nature she reproduces or does she veil that nature? Literally, Eluard seems to close the circle of correspondence inside Nature and, reducing Nature itself to the woman, affirms that, bringing into the world "a body always like," she resembles only herself. But precisely here some despair may dwell. Certainly, nothing more exactly characterizes the amorous excitement than the impression of resemblance that he discovers in the loved one; the loved one is, in effect, the essential resemblance. But Plato was right to claim that we cannot stay there, that this impression must be elucidated and that the lover of resemblances must finally rise to the model valuable in itself, without resembling anything. This means, it is true, that love invites us to surpass love, that it leads us to what is not itself. According to Plato, love is not a God but only an intermediate; he has value only by his goal. Now Breton holds "there is no solution outside of love." [46] But can one be content with love when love does not know what it is love of? Concerned only with love, is not the hope that *Poisson soluble* brought forth in danger of grasping only absence, and ending up in dream and irreality? The poems "à la mystérieuse" of Desnos seem to express a similar despair:

O sorrows of Love!
How necessary you are to me and how dear.
My eyes closing over imaginary tears, my hands reaching
    ceaselessly into the void.[47]

I have dreamed of you so much that you are losing your
    reality.

.   .   .   .

I have dreamed of you so much that my arms used to
    clasping your shadow and crossing on my own chest
    would not fold to the shape of your body, perhaps.

.   .   .   .

I have dreamed of you so much, walked so much, spoken,
    gone to bed with your phantom that all I have
    left perhaps, and still, is to be phantom among
    phantoms . . .[48]

Hence it is necessary, if we do not wish to renounce hope, that the very idea of love be deepened, that its promises be specified, that the beauty and encounter which rouse the lover's excitement deliver up their secret. We know with what passion and with what obstinacy surrealism attempted to discover this secret.

II. Poetry and the Encounter

Light, says Breton, "can be known only three ways: through poetry, freedom, and love." [49] Are these ways different? Accepting the words in their usual meanings we would suppose poetry, freedom, and love to be opposed. Poetry, like freedom, is the power of creating, or at least of conferring a new sense on any object; love on the contrary is passive submission and adoration of what is. But in reality love, poetry, and freedom are reconciled in surrealism by their very ambiguity—each expresses the whole reality of man. Love is forgetfulness of self, but it is not for all that an acceptance of the objective world. It forgets itself only before the loved being, whose face seems to ask that the logical world in which it is held be destroyed and that it be rendered a Universe conformable to itself, the famous "land that resembles you" of Baudelaire.[50] Thus, love is inseparable from revolt; it expresses our fundamental freedom. And this freedom itself is not, in spite of some appearances, a totally arbitrary power of choosing. Rather, it expresses what is most metaphysical in us and what, precisely, the objective and social world strangles, constrains, or at least limits. Breton has always believed in the reality of a deeper self than the conscious one of everyday. At the beginning of *Nadja,* he considers that "what I take for objective manifestations of my existence, manifestations more or less deliberate, are only what happens in the limits of this life of an activity whose true field is totally unknown to me." [51] As for poetry, if everything is apparently permitted there, if the most unexpected juxtapositions are legitimate, it still retains in surrealism the essential sense of an exploration and a revelation. Poetic flashes come to enrich human experience in the manner of premonitions, surrealists hear the revelatory dictation of their unconscious as Paul Eluard "hears" the loved woman; [52] poetic automatism, similar to that of dream, probes into us, into the entire Universe, and gives birth to a sort of prophetic word. Here again the search is ontological: surrealism wishes to abolish "what physically, as they say, keeps us from seeing clearly," and its secret "is in the fact that we are persuaded something is hidden behind" visible objects. [53] Breton declares again that, with Eluard, the choice "of words he assembles, in the order he gives them," "acts through" the poet, rather than being acted upon by him. [54] Obviously, for surrealism it is a question not of giving free rein to a fantasy void of sense but of unveiling the nature of things and of man. Derealization's only function is to make such discoveries possible. If surreality is a "function of our will to complete estrangement of everything," it is because from the "conscious sacrifice" of the primary utility of things "certain transcendent properties are deduced which have connections in another world, given or givable," a world where "lives past, present, and future fuse into one life, which is life." [55]

And certainly the arbitrary seems often to be the source of surrealist invention and even to be sought after for its own sake. It is permissible, says Breton, "to title Poem whatever one obtains by the most gratuitous assemblage possible . . . of headlines and fragments of headlines cut from newspapers." [56] And we know the surrealist games: "Seat yourselves five around a table. Each of you write on a piece of paper, without letting the others see, a noun that will serve as subject of a sentence. Pass this paper to the next person on your left after folding it so as to hide what you have written, meanwhile receiving a similarly folded paper from the person on your right . . . To the noun you cannot see, apply an adjective . . . Proceed in this manner for the verb, then for the noun to serve as direct object, etc. . . . The example, become classic, which gave the game its name, is in the first sentence obtained this way: 'the exquisite cadaver will drink the new wine.'" [57] The surrealist dialogue coupling questions and answers formulated separately is based on similar principles: "What is suicide? —Several deafening bell-tolls." "What is the voluptuousness of living? —It is a marble in a schoolboy's hand." Or again: "If there were no guillotine —Wasps would remove their corsets." [58] "If all horses had magnets for shoes —Lovers' hearts would cease to beat." [59] Several pages of *Les Champs magnétiques* by André Breton and Philippe Soupault are composed thus of two soliloquies intersecting and interrupting each other.[60] While evidently leaving more opportunity for individual choice, the technique of collage is not without analogy with these things. In his 1920 exhibition of collages Max Ernst employed "the photographic element pasted into a drawing or a painting; the drawn or painted element juxtaposed on a photograph; the image cut out and incorporated into a scene or into another image; pure and simple photograph of an arrangement of objects rendered incomprehensible by the photography." [61] After 1920 Max Ernst no longer made anything but pure collages; thus in *La Femme 100 tetês* he drew nothing at all. So Aragon could declare that in all this, "Art has truly ceased to be individual," [62] and could see in the collage a true "trial of personality." "The significant stages of this trial," Aragon writes, "Duchamp drawing a mustache on the Mona Lisa and signing it, Cravan signing a urinal, Picabia signing an ink spot and titling it Holy Virgin, are for me the logical consequences of the initial gesture of collage. What is now maintained on the one hand is the negation of technique, as in collage, and in addition negation of the technical personality; the painter—if he can still be called that—is no longer linked to his painting by a mysterious physical relationship analogous to generation." [63] Surrealist dialogues, games of *cadavre exquis*, collages, tend thus to engender the masterpiece without an author,[64] result of chance and of encounter, masterpiece whose most exact announcement is the famous formula of Lautréamont: "Beautiful as the fortuitous encounter of a sewing machine and an umbrella on a dissecting table."

But it is precisely to this extent that for the surrealists the aesthetic emotion approaches the amorous emotion and becomes inseparable from it. It should not be supposed that the fortuitous encounter is valuable as such or because it is fortuitous. On the contrary, what is astonishing is that, fortuitous in origin, it produces beauty; hence its result appears under the sign of a purposiveness which, however, we know perfectly well did not preside at its birth. In this way, surrealism seems to administer the proof of what it claims when, posing in a new way the eternal problem of inspiration, it affirms that in the poet illumination follows creation. We know how Breton, in this matter, has risen against the "pretended visionary power of the poet." "No," he writes, "Lautréamont, Rimbaud did not see, did not enjoy, *a priori* what they described, which amounts to saying that they did not describe it; they were confined in the dark grooves of being to hear the speaking indistinctly and, while they wrote, understanding no better than we the first time we read them certain completed and completable works. Illumination comes later." [65] Whatever opinion one may have of the process of poetic creation, it is clear that in the surrealist dialogue or the game of *cadavre exquis* the illumination, as Breton says, comes later. From this, we can no longer limit ourselves to saying that the poet is unconsciously inspired, letting a sort of god speak from within him. Now we must either deny or discover that god.

We may search in two ways the source of surrealist illumination. We may see proof there of the power of our spirit, capable of giving value to no matter what and of conferring sense where there is none. Let us take again the surrealist game of question and answer. In order to eliminate all beauty proper to any of the sentences put forward (which was not always done by the surrealists) we shall take examples from our personal exercises. We can agree that from the beginning nothing is any more banal and exact, nothing less poetic or revelatory than the questions and answers that follow. What is a hat? —What we cover our heads with. What is a plate? —A little container from which we eat. What is dawn? —The rise of day. What is a mirror? —What gives us back our image. What is a policeman? —The guardian of order. What is a radiator? —A tube filled with hot water. What is a gaslight? —A streetlamp. What is a dream? —An illusion during sleep. If now we invert by pairs the questions and the answers, we get: "What is a hat? —A little container from which we eat. What is a plate? —What we cover our heads with. What is dawn? —What gives us back our image. What is a mirror? —The rise of day. What is a policeman? —A tube filled with hot water. What is a radiator? —The guardian of order. What is a gaslight? —An illusion during sleep. What is a dream? —A streetlamp." The striking thing here is that none of the answers obtained appears to the spirit as devoid of sense. In order to attain or confer these different senses, the spirit must only change attitudes. The normal answers make sense before its logical attitude. The answers obtained by inversion make sense before its humorous attitude (What is a policeman? —A tube filled with hot water) or lyric attitude (What is a dream? —A streetlamp) or magical attitude (What is dawn? —What gives us back our image) etc. One could conclude from this that spirit draws from its own strength the cause for its solitude; if it can bestow a sense on anything it can never be sure of finding traces of anything other than itself. The order it discovers will always be its own order, the beauty it contemplates always its own beauty. The surrealist experience has often been interpreted this way; if surrealism wishes to bring together in its images the most distant realities, is it not because of its unlimited confidence in the powers of the spirit? Is this not why Dali can call himself "prince of the Catalonian intelligence, colossally rich," [66] and Mesens can write,

> *Would you like a hidden treasure*
> *Here are five fingers*
> *Here is a hand*
> *Here are five fingers and five paths*
> *And here are five hidden treasures.*[67]

In this case, surrealist liberty would be essentially the power to direct oneself wherever seemed good and to create values. Surrealism would justify the axiology of Raymond Polin, for whom man is the creator of values, which have their sense only from him and relative to him.[68]

But surrealist freedom is less free will than fidelity to destiny. This is why it regards poetic illumination less as invention of a meaning than discovery of a presence. Breton insists always on the passivity of spirit, creation seeming of less importance to him than revelation; so the encounters provoked in art often give place to the encounters suffered in life. In any case the two are inseparable, and it is life that gives art its significance and seriousness. At the end of *Nadja* beauty is called convulsive only because it brings into question our relation to the world; the work as a whole has illustrated this point of view by prodding the reader's emotion with the evocation of real encounters—by which the narrative is meant to give, better than any confession borrowing its insights from introspection, the sensation of what Breton "is." Asking, in fact, "Who am I?" and desiring to communicate his response to the reader ("For myself," Breton writes, "I shall continue to live in my glass house" [69]) Breton tries in *Nadja* to relate "the most notable episodes" of his life so that he can conceive it "outside its organic plan, to the same extent to which it is subjected to chance, the smallest as well as the largest, where it eludes fleetingly [his own] influence," where it introduces him into "a world almost forbidden, which is that of things suddenly brought together, of petrifying coincidences, of each individual's own reflexes, harmonies pounded out as if on a piano, flashes that would make us see, but really see, if they were not still more rapid than the others." [70] "I will limit myself here," Breton says again, "to remembering without effort what without resulting from any action on my part nevertheless happened to me." [71] Nothing shows better how Breton puts a premium only on receptivity. His aim is not to establish the power of spirit conferring sense on encounters; on the contrary, he expects the sense from the signs, and it is with the image of the "message" that *Nadja* ends. [72] We can see how little the proposed problem is literary or, more exactly, how much the poetic emotion is reduced to being only a particular case of the uneasiness man can feel before any "signal." Breton is seated with Nadja, Place Dauphine. Nadja is glancing "along the buildings. —Do you see, down there, that window? It is black, like all the others. Keep looking at it. In a minute it will light up. It will be red. The minute passes. The window lights up. It has, in fact, red curtains." [73] Elsewhere, at the Tuileries, before a fountain, Nadja repeats the analogy expressed in a vignette in Berkeley's *Three Dialogues Between Hylas and Philonous,* which Breton was reading, an analogy very seldom noted, I should add, between the movement of the water of a fountain and that of human thoughts. [74] Here are encounters not easily explained by simple recourse to coincidence and which, like the encounters of art that produce beauty, engender an excitement that seems the sign of an objective purposiveness or, at least, the trace of a meaning of which we are not the only creator. This purposiveness, this meaning, presuppose—within the real—an order that is their source. What order, distinct from the order of everyday causality, does it signify?

This problem, more than any other, has preoccupied surrealism. "Can you say," Breton and Eluard ask in *Minotaure,* "what has been the main encounter of your life? To what extent has this encounter given you, does this encounter give you, the impression of being fortuitous? of being necessary?" I myself responded to this inquiry in the spirit of a defiant rationalism:

"1) With a woman whom I love.

"2) This encounter gave me and gives me the impression of being necessary (in other words, I cannot decide to consider it as an encounter). But such an impression is subject to criticism. It arises first of all from the fact that the spirit tends to regard all things as necessary. Besides, the loved woman holding sway over my memory and my consciousness, my remembrances being recalled only in proportion as she calls for them, the events of my life being retained by me only if she is involved in them, my past can only appear to me as announcing the coming of this woman, my present life seems to me to have no other sense but what she gives it. But I see in all that only a rational exigency *a priori* and a mechanism of the passions. Having no valid reason to believe in the necessity of my encounter with the loved woman, I hold this encounter for a true encounter; I consider it as fortuitous." [75]

But clearly my statement was not concerned with any fact analogous to those Breton evokes. Joë Bousquet gave to the same inquiry a troubling reply. In the spring of 1917, in the Chemin des Dames, he fired, against the advice of his soldiers, on two Germans, thus provoking a riposte and combat in which one of his men, Sergeant Canet, was wounded by a bullet in his vertebral column. Sergeant Canet, who died the next day in an ambulance, leveled at Bousquet a reproach full of hate: "To the grave, you'll send me to the grave!" A year later, Bousquet sustained a similar injury, which confined him to his bed for the rest of his life. Bousquet adds that he was, nevertheless, able to give his life a new meaning thanks to the friendship of Claude Estève, born in a village in Aude called Canet. This Estève himself, who was likewise a marvelous friend to me, died at the same period in which Bousquet was writing the reply for *Minotaure*. And Bousquet's life was, more than any other, filled with signs of this sort. Bousquet often assured me that several episodes in *La Tisane de sarments* contained nothing fictional. For instance, he was accustomed to imagine death in the form of a girl who gathered vine shoots. Now having once noticed in a girl friend he had made up as a peasant a resemblance to a gatherer of vine shoots, and having told her this (without, of course, revealing to her "the thought behind this exclamation"), he beheld her go pale and heard her say, "I didn't think it would be necessary for me to pass by the cemetery. I'll never dare." And the next day the "poor little thing" was run over by a truck carrying "a coffin, an empty coffin." [76]

Nothing would be served by multiplying such examples. The important thing would be to discover the sense attributable to these events. In *Nadja* Breton professes to be only a "haggard witness." [77] These events, he says again, "each time present all the appearances of a signal, without our being able to say just what they are signals of." [78] And Breton limits himself to concluding that in full solitude he still enjoys "unlikely complicities," and that he is not "alone at the helm of the ship." [79] This is enough not to attribute to him the idea of a liberty that would be absolute choice by the subject of the way he will engage in life. But it is not enough to decide if his philosophy must be taken for a subjectivism, indeed a psychologism, in which the subject, in contact only with himself, can receive only messages emanating in reality from himself, or for a magic realism in which the encounters must be held as marks of a transcendent exteriority. In *L'Amour fou* Breton seems to hesitate between these two ways. Only, he writes in fact, "the precise and absolutely conscientious reference to the emotional state of the subject at the moment such events are produced can furnish a real basis for appreciation." [80] And on the other hand, pointing out the "need for holding the unfolding of exterior life as independent of what constitutes spiritually my individuality," it is, he adds, "strangely difficult to admit that this spectacle is suddenly organized as if for me alone and apparently no longer tends toward anything but conformity to the representation I have already had of it." [81] Breton thus seems to believe in "the triggering of a contact, a dazzling one, between man and the world of things." Why, however, wanting to make his thought more precise, does he declare that the word "revelatory," which he has employed, is not used "in its metaphysical meaning," but that only it seems to him "strong enough to express the unparalleled emotion" it has been given him to feel? [82] Of course, Breton often uses the word "metaphysical" in a pejorative sense and has always loathed having his experience confounded with a mystical one, including that to which the hermeticists seem to invite us. For this reason it is hard to follow Carrouges all the way when he sees in surrealist poetry a continuation of alchemy.[83] The "alchemy of the word" dear to Rimbaud could not enforce a direct action on matter, and when Breton declares that we must take these words "literally" [84] he is aware for all that how language manipulates only the names of things, never the things themselves. The transformation expected from alchemy of the word remains transformation of our consciousness, "recreation of a state which has no need to envy mental alienation." [85] This is why, far from assimilating his search to that for the philosophers' stone, Breton assimilates rather the search for the philosophers' stone to a freeing of the imagination. "The philosophers' stone is nothing else than what permits man's imagination to take flagrant revenge on all things." [86] It remains that being content with a transformation purely mental, considering only subjective emotion, surrealism would rob the encounters of all their sense as signals and would be able to see only illusion in the impression of discovery that they arouse. Once more, the surrealist expectation would be expectation without an object.

It is not enough, in resolving such a problem, to invoke

the famous supreme point where the subjective and the objective become identical for surrealism. This would be, in our view, to confuse the surrealist experience with a mystical, superhuman experience, to suppose that it places us on a level of reality of which our subjective reality and the objective world are simply two aspects. "Everything leads us to believe," Breton writes, "that there exists a certain point in the spirit at which life and death, the real and the imaginary, the past and the future, the communicable and the incommunicable, the high and the low cease to be perceived as contradictory. Now it is vain to search for any other motive in surrealist activity than the hope of determining that point." [87] No doubt we must admit with Carrouges that this idea "comes from the Hermetic tradition," "is found in the Kabbalah and plays an essential role in the *Zohar*." [88] But it is difficult to agree with him that this Hermetic idea has passed into surrealism without a complete change of nature, becoming "the fundamental cornerstone of surrealist cosmology," [89] or to consider that here surrealism limits itself to suppressing the "divine presence hidden in the background" [90] and secularizing the idea according to which there would be a "point of origin for the Creation, the point of action at which God created the world and at which all is contained *ab ovo*." [91] Breton has not only secularized the mystical idea of a supreme point. From cosmological he seems to have made it psychological: does he not speak of a supreme point "in the spirit"? And Breton gives as the aim of surrealist activity, not the discovery, but—which is quite different —"hope of determining that point." "I have spoken," he will say in *L'Amour fou*, "of a certain sublime point in the mountain. There was never any question of my going to live at that point. It would, besides, at that moment have ceased to be sublime and I myself to be a man." [92] Never have Breton's humanism and lucidity found more exact expression. It is only from man's perspective, a perspective that Breton has never claimed to go beyond, that we should pose the question of so-called "objective chance." [93] And after all it is only from this perspective that the question can be posed if its mystery is, as Breton thinks, that of "the encounter of an external causality with an internal purposiveness." [94] In the ontological illumination, there would no longer be an encounter between external causality and internal purposiveness, but identity. It is important, thus, not to reverse the order of stages. Breton starts with the encounters, he is stunned by them, he tries to interpret them. It is by starting from them that he hopes to determine the supreme point. They give him a sign of it. But Breton's critical spirit forbids him to confound what signifies with what is signified. Breton does not know what Being is. He does not know in advance even what will fulfill his desire or, for example, that the spoon found and bought at the flea market will be the object to respond to his need for possessing "the lost slipper of Cinderella." [95] He expects and sometimes avows that only expectation "is magnificent." [96] And in fact the encounter, like love, if it is revelation, is still expectation, since we do not know what it really signifies. Is it the very reality of the world? Is it the mirage of our desire? Expectation is still maintained in the surrealist experience, it remains at the center of the ravishment of discovery; it cannot be altogether fulfilled, since it cannot yield its place to what would really be knowledge. Some would prefer, no doubt, to see Breton decide, state finally what he waits for, affirm that he has discovered or despaired of discovering it, pronounce the encounters either objectively revelatory or purely subjective and illusory. Breton holds his peace and continues to question himself. Is this weakness? Is it strength? Are we witnessing the failure of surrealism, the definitive deception of its first hope? Or are we arriving, on the contrary, in recording its ambiguity, at a comprehension of what in its message is most authentic and most profound?

We have certainly arrived at the essential problem that, philosophically, surrealism poses. But what powers, what ecstasies (perhaps also what laziness) invite us to go around it! Before their temptation, the project of this book itself seems questionable: is not translating surrealism philosophically to rob it of its reality? How much easier to reread *Nadja,* giving in to its spell, not to decide if the dream opens reality to us or signifies only itself, and when the window in the Place Dauphine turns red, when the fountain in the Tuileries sketches the vignette from the *Three Dialogues Between Hylas and Philonous,* to be moved without replying. Thus, no doubt, Breton wanders across Paris, predicting the shops that will advertise "Wood & Coal," attends, at the Théâtre des Deux-Masques, that strange play without a conclusion in which when the closet is opened the gory body of a child "appears head downward and tumbles onto the stage," [97] hears finally without quite understanding the mysterious phrases of Nadja: "Horrible! Do you see what is passing through the trees? The blue and the wind, the blue wind." [98] "Not there . . . But tell me, why must you go to prison? What will you have done? I have been in prison too. Who was I? Centuries ago. And you, then, who were you?" [99] Will one who has participated in the surrealist state be able to find a different expression for what he has already been given? How will he escape, in order to talk about it, this interpenetration of dream, waking, poetry, madness, whose fusing announces, promises, troubles, but does not allow knowing? Will every step toward clarity not be abstraction and betrayal? And, nevertheless, we have one encouraging sign. Breton did not come to love Nadja. Nadja loved Breton, whom she took for the Sun.[100] Thus, in *Nadja* itself madness aspires to lucidity and seems to predict that the riches it holds can be fully revealed only in becoming conscious and, if one may say so, on the level of reason. This reason is not technological or scientific reason, which surrealism has never ceased regarding as incapable of containing the richness of the World, but a new reason in which man as a whole may find his image again, a reason from which surrealism has never stopped asking—like the dying Goethe—more light. Surrealism has opened the road for the steps of that reason, not as it has sometimes believed by borrowing from Hegel an irrelevant dialectic, but in showing that contact with the immediate contains it own clarity. And clarity is always the same, whether we search for it in chance encounters, in poetry, or in love. Before surrealism, astonishment at encounters was relegated to superstition, love to psychology, the poetic emotion to literature. Surrealism has established that these states all contain the same hope, they all reveal in analogous ways the relation between man and the real.

III. Lucidity

"Who goes there? Who goes there? Is it you Nadja? Is it true that the beyond, all the beyond, is in this life? I do not understand you. Who goes there? Is it I alone? Is it myself?" We have quoted this passage already. But it is hard to resist bringing it up again, since in our view it goes farther than any other in uniting the pathetic with lucid desire to know. Breton, wanting to recover all man's powers, wanting to renounce nothing of human reality, establishes here that man is interrogation, is—as has been said since then—a questioning of the World and of himself. He is expectation, not discovery. Breton rejects all determinations, keeping at the very heart of his faith in the unique love something of the availability that made him write in *Les Pas perdus*, "Every night I left the door of my hotel room wide open, in hopes of waking at last by the side of a woman I had not chosen." [101] He refuses all dogmatisms, scientific or religious. His expectation may well pass, as Carrouges says, for "a profane form of eternal hope." [102] But it is a hope without faith, without adherence to any contents whatever. With this in mind we must not be satisfied with admitting that surrealism does not always solve its problems. We must realize that this absence of response alone reveals man's authenticity. Is not every response an alienation of freedom and betrayal of that total man for whom surrealism seems to wish to witness? Is not man, prior to all language, contact with the other than himself, other than he can ever completely reduce and know? Is he not the sign in this World of an unknown presence? Surrealism, wanting to restore to us total consciousness and to give it to us in its original purity, can only rid it of all the hypotheses which are mixed into the expression it has formerly given of itself. Among them there is the hypothesis of God and also the theories and laws that scientific knowledge has been forging ceaselessly, interposing between man and man this objective world where desire does not recognize itself. If surrealism takes sides with childhood against the adults who mistreat or teach children, with madness against those who lock up madmen,[103] with "admirable love" against "sordid life," [104] it is because it believes adult, social, everyday reason, not content with oppressing man, betrays him. Moreover, any consciousness man takes of himself appears insufficient with respect to his exigency and his reality. It is in this sense that P.-O. Lapie can write, "Here, not only is liberty not a permission given by society, it is not even a permission given by man himself. It is not subject to his own, his conscious will; it comes from him." [105] From whence the surrealist grasp of the real, where anything oppressed by normal thought finds its chance—surrealism does not like losing reason, it likes everything that reason makes us lose. And what reason makes us lose is not merely a set of unreasonable hypotheses; it is also that primitive authenticity that is the absence of hypotheses, and essential questioning.

No doubt it is difficult to see the link between the conception of man as interrogation and the conception of man as totality, which seem by turns to be that of surrealism. But the difficulty arises from wishing to resolve on a conceptual level a problem whose solution can only be an experience, the unspeakable and pristine experience of human reality. Spinoza, trying to reconcile, on the level of God, unity and totality, enunciated the principle: *omnis determinatio negatio.* We believe that in order to seize the reality of man we must take up that proposition again. For all determination of man, though at first it seems to enrich him, limits and then negates the particular reality that is his. Nothing shows better how this reality is not that of a thing (for a thing is enriched by its determinations), but that of a freedom. Descartes draws his *sum* from his *cogito* and *cogito* from doubt, which is negation of the world of objects. Man's being appears thus as the very being of that negation. Derealizing, anti-objective, anti-dogmatic negation and affirmation of man are likewise linked in Breton. What illuminates things is man, and he illuminates them only because he is not a thing but absolute availability. With this single condition, man can be light and light on all things. We must not search here for dialectic subtlety; dialectic is adding up; it finds the absolute "at the goal," in a synthesis that retains the set of determinations that it has gone beyond. With surrealism, we are at the beginning and at the base: the unity of man is discovered in the immediate; that is why it gives itself to us as a nothing, that is why it has everything to expect from the World and accepts any adventure. So Breton refuses any specialization whatever. "Surrealism," he writes, "should not be considered as existing, except in the *a priori* nonspecialization of its effort." [106] And I think this conception of man defines surrealism better than does its vision of the world. I have some trouble following Carrouges when he inserts the surrealist project into the context of the great Promethean project by which man would annex all religious territory,[107] as well as Pastoureau when he seems to expect above all from surrealism a *Weltanschauung* destined to replace the Christian vision of the

Universe.[108] Pastoureau, it is true, speaks elsewhere of a *Weltanschauung* of ambivalence.[109] Now the notion of ambivalence brings us back to human reality, a reality that admits of contradictions—not because it surmounts them dialectically, but because it is preexistent to all the theses and antitheses that reason can oppose, and which have meaning only in its regard.

The admiration of many surrealists for Heraclitus thus seems explicable. "Heraclitus," Char writes, "is of all men the one who, refusing to break up the prodigious question, conducted it by gestures into the intelligence and habits of man without attenuating its fire, interrupting its complexity, compromising its mystery, oppressing its juvenility. He knew that the truth is noble and that the image that reveals it is tragedy. He was not content to define liberty, he discovered it could not be uprooted. . ." [110] And Char, though he has quit surrealism, has kept its sense of man. The sentence that Pierre Berger places at the beginning of his study,[111] "If we inhabit a lightning bolt, it is the heart of the eternal," expresses at once the precariousness and the preeminence that surrealism always grants to man—and which are, as it were, the secret of all atheist poetry and doubtless of all poetry. For all poetry is atheist at its base, atheist as it is irrational or nonscientific. We do not claim, it goes without saying, that every poet is an atheist, or that atheism is true, or even that the unknown, that Being that all poetry and all art designate is not God. But whether or not it is God is for the philosopher to decide. In saying that it is God, in naming it, in determining it, the poet goes beyond his proper knowledge and ceases to be a poet; he sounds a theoretical affirmation that is no longer in his province and which therefore can appear poetically only as arbitrary. Of course, classical poetry presents all at once, as if confused, poetic evidence and also objective significance which, already, specifies and denatures that evidence. But we are touched by it and hold its language to be poetic only while perceiving, under the rational sense that forces itself on us, the other sense, the original sense. Imagine, says Roxane to Bajazet, "that your breath lasts only while I love you." [112] Logically that signifies: It is in my power to have you put to death, but the love I bear you keeps me from carrying this out. Anyone can see that if she expressed herself thus, her speech would be poetically empty. Roxane's words, thus, have beyond their logical sense a poetic sense that will be found again in the surrealist theme of love creating the being it loves—at which point it might be remarked that this is, strictly speaking, the literal sense, not an interpretation of the line. Likewise, when Racine writes:

> *Star of which our sun is but gross shadow,*
> *Holy day, that lends our day its brightness* [113]

it is beyond argument that he wishes intellectually to signify that the reality of the World depends on the divine Word. But that sun becoming a shadow, that day seeming all of a sudden to be perceived only in a mirror and borrowing its light from another day which would alone be the true day—these dissolve the ordinary world in an atmosphere that is exactly that of surrealist de-realization. This is why the atheism of the surrealists and their confidence in a single poetry are one and the same thing. No doubt this link, this unity, has been masked rather than revealed by many an excess; such as Marcel Noll's writing to Stanislas Fumet, "Baudelaire a Catholic? a believer? Then how could he have been a poet?" [114] But we will see the unity when we realize that it is in attempting to create poetry not objectively interpretable that surrealism brought to light the essence of all poetry. Benjamin Péret played an essential role in this purification, with his obvious images void of any logical sense, like "the strident cry of red eggs," [115] images discouraging any explication in rational or scholarly style. Here the absurd becomes irrefutable truth. If, in fact, one claims that poetry is a lie, has he not confused poetry with an interpretation that he mixes with its primary expression, reaching for it on a level where it is already rationalized? So Edouard Maynial, commenting on Nerval's line:

And the fatal grotto with its imprudent guests

figures that the poet is mixing up the grotto of the Cumean Sibyl or Grotta d'Averno (which Maynial says he intends) with the Grotta del Cane at Bagnoli, which is deadly "because of escaping carbonic gas." [116] Explanatory commentaries on poetry seem to me to be worth just what that one is; the most one can say of them is that they are beside the point. Etiemble, one of the freest spirits of our time, has sought to discover the origin and trace back to its genesis all the errors promulgated about Rimbaud.[117] I believe with him that one can begin to understand a poet only after rejecting all the images that have been built up around him, all the interpretations that have been given. But I also think that in the work of Rimbaud there is no true sense to be opposed to all the false ones Etiemble is denouncing, none that could be defined by reference to what Rimbaud might, as a matter of fact, have meant. More exactly, what Rimbaud meant appears to me to have only anecdotal interest and concerns only the man Rimbaud, and I think it matters little to know what it was. "Real life is absent. We are not in the world," [118] Rimbaud wrote. Does he want to signify that true life is that of the Christian paradise? Does he condemn the social alienation that makes man a slave? I have no idea. But I know that if Rimbaud had been content to say, "I want to go to heaven," or "I hope for everything from the society of the future," his declarations would have no more worth than those proffered daily by revolutionaries or writers of catechisms. If the words of Rimbaud are moving to this extent, it is because they recover an absolute truth, on the level of fundamental experience, revealing this existence separated from Being that is human existence.

And this truth, nonobjective, nonhypothetical, is the source of all the derived affirmations that one can draw out of them—one of which may possibly have satisfied the clear consciousness of Rimbaud. Would Christians aspire to heaven, politicos to revolution, if they were not first of all men and drew their certitudes from a first consciousness which before any hypothesis, before any formulated hope, is consciousness of dissatisfaction and expectation? Only this consciousness is certain, only its language is without prevarication and falsity, and only it is original. Any of the limited senses one can attribute to Rimbaud's words, even if it were historically established that Rimbaud had wanted to give such and such a one to his words, refer back to that indefinable reality that is man and of which poetry is the direct expression. Thus, poetry says all or, if you like, says nothing; it is certainly not content to say something, saying something being always to speak in reference to objects and thus to quit the level of human reality as unity and totality. To give an intellectual sense to the words of a poet is to abandon authenticity for discourse, being for object, the certain for the probable. Poetry and the critical metaphysics whose project it retrieves cannot lie. They speak Being and man in proportion as they refuse objective language and with it all hypothesis and all alienation.

It must come as no surprise then that surrealism has believed itself capable of judging by the norms of poetry all human affirmations whether religious, occult, scientific, or political. Certainly, it does not reject anything positive in any of these affirmations. In religion Breton, steering completely away from Voltaire's sterilizing criticism, seems to us to retain adoration and also the idea that the Principle situated on the other side of things is of the nature of our consciousness or of our life. He feels led toward the Christian heretics,[119] and Monnerot has with great penetration and restraint compared "gnostics and surrealists." [120] Occultism tempts surrealism: "The process of artistic discovery," Breton writes, is "supported by the same form and the same means of progression as transcendental magic."[121] From science surrealism retains all the light, even when that light seems to dissolve the wonders that attend its own plan. We may be astonished to hear Breton, after having defined surrealism as the "mode of creating a collective myth,"[122] declare to the students at Yale, "We need to sweep with searchlights and then try resolutely to cleanse that immense and dark region of ourselves where myths swell out of all proportion," and ask for "an intervention in mythic life which would take first, on the grandest scale, the shape of a clean-up."[123] We are forgetting the use the surrealists have always made of Freudian methods. Far from fearing that psychoanalytic explanations would dissipate the excitement of the marvelous or disqualify the promises of coincidence or, finally, reduce the mystery of beauty to an illusion of our desire, Breton patiently interprets his dreams,[124] explicates the force of Lautréamont's images by referring to "the key of sexual symbols,"[125] tends even to clarify encounters and the state of ecstatic surprise into which they plunge us by invoking a sort of partial selection operated by us within the infinite richness of the given exterior. He notes that in such experiences, just as in dream, "desire, which in its essence remains the same, seizes whatever happens to serve its satisfactions."[126] And we have seen Breton hold over from Marxism its critical method and its hope of man's liberation. But he refuses everything which in religious, occultist, scientific, or Marxist affirmations seems to him to limit man, to constrain him, to specify him. The sexual prohibitions of Christianity seem intolerable to him; occult beliefs seem dubious—*Arcane 17* holds "every reservation" on the "very principle" of esoterism.[127] To the objectivistic inspiration of science, to its "positivistic realism" and "narrow reason," Breton opposes "a reason true and without eclipses"[128] and "appetite for a universal knowledge to be rediscovered."[129] Lastly, to the Hegelian-Marxist theory seeing in labor the fundamental relation between man and Nature, he holds up the ravishments of love and the light of expectation. "The living we call 'earned' regains the aspect it had for us in childhood: it again takes the form of life *lost*. Lost to games, lost to love." [130] "There is no use living if one has to work. The event from which each man has the right to expect the revelation of the sense of his own life ... is not the reward of labor." [131] In such remarks, it is man, seized by poetry in its pristine, unalienated clarity that makes obvious the insufficiency of all ideas, all images, and even of the World in which one wishes to enclose it. In *Légitime défense* Breton, after having made the communist program his, remarks that "there are in us some vacancies that all our ... hope in the triumph of communism cannot fill; is not man unfailingly the enemy of man? will boredom end, except with the end of the world? is not any assurance of life or honor vain? etc." He assumes that the communist faith, "like any other, requires a certain act of grace." [132] And, indeed, some grace is always necessary to bend the infinite demand of the human spirit till it recognizes its object in some determination, in some finitude. The faith that brings Christians to confess that the man Jesus is God requires the acceptance of a similar limitation. In this sense Breton rejects all grace; nothing of what may be offered to our experience or defined by our thought can fulfill his expectation. Human desire surpasses every object, is satisfied by no faith; its appeal is limitless.

Marcel Raymond, after having remarked that our civilization, established "on a rational and positive conception of the universe and of life ... has separated man from the universe and from a part of himself," declares that the poets, "to the extent that they make the poetic act a vital operation, fulfill a compensatory function." [133] We could say the same for metaphysicians, if we could suppose them to have an audience in society. Modern metaphysics was born with Descartes and can be understood only as a reaction to the upheaval brought about

in the consciousness of men by the arrival of technological science. In the Middle Ages objects were taken
for beings; Nature went deeper and deeper until it
reached God, each thing had some value and fulfilled
some goal. Man could thus love the sensible world that
was offered to him, a world not, of course, divinized, but
still not separated from divine truth, to which it testified
and toward which it aided him to rise. The technological
project, on the contrary, devalorizes a Nature that man
wishes to subject, to which he can no longer attribute
true being or proper goals. It engenders mechanical
science, in which the World's events are despoiled of
their qualities and reduced to displacements of matter.
But while the materialists held to this despairing conception and reduced being to that inhuman nature, which
they forgot was the product of one of man's projects,
Descartes opposed the World, considered as a fable, with
the Being of God, whose sign is our consciousness. This
Being is so little reducible to the paltriness of extended
space that, quite the reverse, we can raise ourselves to
the thought of it only by understanding that the structure
of the physical world—even when it seems rationally
necessary to us—is the totally arbitrary product of his
will. By other routes, but with equal force, Kant will
affirm the irreducibility of Being to any object known
scientifically. Still, metaphysics is negative; it affirms being without qualifying it. It lets man know the world of
mechanics is not Being, but it does not replace that
world with any other. Human consciousness is thus unsatisfied by such ascetic compensation. It desires to grasp
again in all things the Being that science kidnapped.
From whence the flowering, ever since the seventeenth
century, of the marvelous: at first shy and taking the
form of faërie, the marvelous becomes in romanticism
the very source of a poetry that, far from simply opposing science, claims to outdo science on its own ground,
to become a source of knowledge and of a knowledge
deeper and closer to Being than scientific know-how.

Scientific knowledge separates the self from the universe which it sets up as object. Poetic knowledge cancels that separation and allows a fusion thanks to which the human subject, which positive know-how condemned to solitude, penetrates all the secrets of the World. Dream and the unconscious reclaim their rights, thought participates in all the movements of the real, man feels in himself universal life. Thus, there is realized, as Marcel Raymond says, "the dream of a magical universe where man would not feel himself distinct from things, where spirit would reign without intermediary over phenomena, outside any rational track." [134] But we believe that in this general movement of modern poetry surrealism occupies a very special place as intermediary between confident romanticism and metaphysical criticism. It insists less on the knowledge poetry can procure than on its power of subjective transformation. It accepts psychoanalysis and by it reduces cosmological illumination to the subjectivity of desire. It pronounces only discreetly on the bearing of its experiences. It joins to their excitement a critical interrogation. It doubts and, by this doubt, it becomes humanistic even more than it becomes a magical cosmology. As in critical metaphysics so in surrealism: man is the unique basis of truth and of judgment. Surrealism is not then, as some would have it, an exaggerated romanticism. It is not content with continuing Novalis, von Arnim or Blake. It submits the romantic experience to the criterion of lucidity. And the spontaneous and original language to which surrealism has recourse is considered as expressing, still more than the mysteries of Nature, man's unconscious.

In the name of man, we have seen surrealism reject all transcendence—that of God, that of society and its constraints, that of matter considered as self-sufficient. But man would be betrayed if reduced to himself; once more his consciousness would be confused with a thing. Man is contact with the Other, and it is in this sense that he can love. I do not believe we can agree with Breton that the idea that love comes to an end when the loved being "is no longer hidden" must be "attributed to . . . an after-effect, usually atavistic, of religious education, which sees to it that the human being is always ready to postpone the possession of truth and happiness." [135] Since love is addressed not to an object of thought but to a being, something will always be hidden; every being is free and contains some infinity. It is, therefore, inexhaustible and, strictly speaking, unknowable. In this sense religion is right to warn us that nothing given can altogether fulfill our expectation; far from deceiving us on this point, it witnesses a perfect fidelity to man's reality. Now surrealism, in most of its affirmations, comes back to this fidelity. Surrealist hope if it appears at first in Aragon's term, "immense and naive," [136] soon begins to show the melancholy that Giorgio de Chirico expresses with such force in his painting "Melancholy and Mystery of a Street." [137] After singing the "marvelous noon," Crevel adds, "But it is late, mysterious woman. You are passing by. We must say adieu. Tomorrow you leave again for your primal fogs." [138] So being is hidden. For man, the words "it is late" have meaning. And the adieu of the surrealists does not manage to become an *à Dieu*. In *Arcane 17* Breton declares that man prides himself wrongly on "being the great predestined one of creation." "All that evolutionary theory," he writes, "has been able to reveal to him of his origin and of the general biological necessities that assign a period to the duration even of his species remains in effect empty words. He persists in seeing and acting as if those revelations which would wound his pride had never taken place. The very reserves philosophers have taught him to make concerning the capacity of his understanding appear in his remarks only as a matter of form and do nothing to dissuade him in his heart of hearts from disposing final causes as if they had something necessarily to do with him." [139] In such remarks the surrealist hope is separated from religious hope; far from wanting to go past hope toward a romantic illusion of fusion between man and Being, it wishes to make itself more restrained, more reserved, to limit itself still more, to accept the measures and criteria of knowing.

I have often in these pages compared the surrealist poets to Plato, Descartes, and Kant. This is not, I hope it is clear, in order to reduce everything I like to a unity. It is rather because I have managed to like only those who refuse to make affirmations beyond their certitude, those who recognize throughout their discourse that they are men. In Breton and in the authentic philosophers is found the same truth, the same fidelity to man-as-interrogation, man-as-question. Dogmatism gives way to quest for being. Poetry, though it delivers us from technological narrowness—though by revealing how an object may be invested with multiple meanings it gives evidence for positivism's fragility and the radical poverty of a vision of the World as physics—does not for all that pretend to hand over all the keys or open all doors for us. It does not become a new dogmatism; its cause remains that of our freedom. It is as men that we follow its path, that we try to comprehend its revelations, that we make an effort—thanks to it—to decipher life "like a cryptogram." [140] The source of the surrealist movement was hope. Before the difficulties of its road, surrealism had chosen neither the illusion of discovery nor the pessimism of abandon. It has risen to greater consciousness. It has become reflection on hope.

Chapter Four

Imagination

I. The Imaginary and the Real

Hope opposes to the given real a better state that it imagines. "It is hope or despair," Eluard writes, "that will determine for the waking dreamer—for the poet— the action of his imagination." [1] Reflecting on hope is thus an attempt to discover the relation between the real and the imaginary. Surrealism having denounced "the artificial character of the old antinomies," [2] and having proposed to "reduce these oppositions wrongly presented as insurmountable, deplorably hollowed in the course of ages and which are the real alembics of suffering, op- position of madness and supposed reason . . . of dream and action . . . of mental representation and physical per- ception," [3] one could believe that it takes the relation of real and imaginary to be pure identity. This would be forgetting surrealist lucidity; surrealism uses only "volun- tary hallucination," [4] and if it labors "toward making the distinction between subjective and objective lose its necessity and its value," this is while "sheltered from any madness." [5] The total union of the real and the imaginary, yielding "shadow and prey fused into a single flash," [6] is certainly presented by the surrealists as a sort of ideal. But it can be attained only at that sublime point Breton avows to be superhuman. Surrealism is therefore most often content with "throwing a conducting line between the too separated worlds of waking and sleep, of interior and exterior reality," [7] with describing and analyzing states whose "analogy" with the state of dreaming is so close one cannot fail to be "struck" by it.[8] But the tension remains. There is no definitive solution that would permit man an untroubled repose. More exactly, there is such a solution only for those who, renouncing hope and thereby the imaginary, make everyday reality the measure of their lives. Breton sometimes finds himself envying the people who frolic Sundays on the banks of the Marne. "It is after all for these people," he writes, "that in the woods there are strawberries." [9] In surrealism, on the contrary, the imaginary comes ceaselessly to break the framework of the given, to surpass it, to evoke an inaccessible to which the real itself must, nevertheless, be compared. "There is no model," Eluard writes, "when one is looking for what he has never seen." [10] "The imagination has no instinct for imitation. It is the spring and the torrent that one does not remount." [11] From the moment man imagines, he no longer coincides with the world or with himself. And no more slumber is permitted him.

But what must we understand by *imagination?* Descartes condemns the imagination because it seems to him to participate in the falsity of sensible knowledge, Pascal because he sees in it a spontaneous power of synthesis. Voltaire distinguishes an imagination that reproduces from one that invents, Malebranche distinguishes that which depends on the soul from that which depends on the body. In effect the term "imagination" designates the most diverse operations and states: hypnagogic states, delirium, dreams, aesthetic creation, technical invention, or scientific discovery. Sometimes imagination imposes on us and seems to deceive us, as in hallucination or dream. Sometimes it is the instrument of our progress toward truth or self-mastery. Has imagination then a unity? Is it an attitude? A state? Do images exist, or must we speak only of an imagining consciousness? What parts of it must we accord to spiritual activity and spiritual passivity? And what is the force that, present in us, is not entirely us, which delivers us from the given and yet imposes itself on our clear consciousness? These difficulties concerning the psychological nature of imagination will be found in surrealist questioning. But the surrealists, concerned with the import of imagination as well as with its essence, ask also what is its relation to the real. Should we say that imagination constructs or that it reveals? Jacques Hérold poses the problem: "Breton says that imagination is what tends to become real.[12] Imagination is also what is, but unknown." [13] Following Giordano, according to whom "it is inconceivable that our imagination and our thought surpass Nature and that no reality corresponds to this continual possibility of new spectacle," taking up Nerval's idea that "human imagination has invented nothing not true in this world or some other," [14] Breton declares in connection with the "mental landscape" characteristic of the paintings of Yves Tanguy: "Those who in order to reassure themselves persist in talking about a submarine atmosphere (or some other kind) simply forget how the artistic imagination's faculty of deployment is intimately related to the variety of Cosmic phenomena. When, for example, in New York the superb phenomenon known as the northern lights was revealed to me, everything went as if Tanguy's skies were being unrolled at a vertiginous pace, this signifies that the spirit of Tanguy (who had never perceived this sight any more than I had) is in permanent communication with the terrestrial magnetism." [15] Thus, it is on the level of the imagination that we must pose the problem of surrealist subjectivism or objectivism, of the purely psychological bearing or, on the contrary, the cosmological revelation of poetry. Does imagination create a real that is proper to it? Does it express a real unknown to us? In surrealism there is a way that leads from the imaginary to the real and a way that quits the real to go to the imaginary. Can we follow both at once? Is their duality only apparent, or does it lead us once again to sundering?

The surrealist idea that "the imaginary is what tends to become real" [16] is calculated on the causality of desire. Desire tends in effect to realize what it imagines. But surrealism did not perhaps at first recognize desire as the source of that invasion of man by images that seem to impose on him, frighten him, constrain him. Those images were troubling before they were discovered to be results of deeper tendencies. When Breton, repeating Baudelaire's words, notes that surrealist images, like those of opium, are offered to man "spontaneously, despotically," [17] when he is moved by a subtitle in the film *Nosferatu* ("When he got to the other side of the bridge, the phantoms came to meet him"),[18] when he gives himself over to automatic dictation or begins to listen to the phrases that tap "on the window," [19] he no doubt knows and accepts Freud's idea that any dream is a realized desire. But more directly yet, he is adopting a theory which dominated philosophical teaching until about 1935, the theory according to which imagination is a "realizing" faculty, images tending of themselves to impose on us and presenting themselves as real.[20] This theory, an offshoot of Cartesianism, is found in philosophies as disparate as those of Taine and Bergson. For Taine and for Bergson, in fact, images possess their own force, tending toward expression, and the problem is understanding, not why certain images are realized, but why not all are. Taine invokes here the "reductive" power of sensation which, more intense and stronger than the image, stops it from being given as real. Bergson has recourse to the selective activity of the body, conditioned by the necessities of action. The Cartesians, posing normatively the same question, had for their part tried to oppose the control of reason to the invasion of images always menacing our consciousness. And doubtless the surrealists have, quite the contrary, taken care to remove anything opposed to the free return of images: norms of a logical reason, care for utility, moral censure. But in reversing the table of values of the Cartesian philosophy, they accept its theoretical conception and its psychological schema. They admit then, more or less explicitly, the postulates of this conception: identity of sensation and image, proper existence of images, power of actualization inherent in the image. To my mind many surrealist affirmations cannot be explained apart from these postulates. Thus, speaking of the characters in Achim von Arnim, Breton declares that they merely reproduce "certain properties of optical images that oscillate between virtuality and reality." He notes that for the German romantics objects "know in fact no stability between the real and the imaginary" and that, moreover, artistic creation "will no doubt never permit a total discrimination between these two solutions—the real and the imaginary." [21]

But in the same text Breton perceives the link between such conceptions and what he calls "the grandiose error of Fichte," "which consists of believing in the attribution of being (of objectivity) by thought, in sensation extended in space." His concern for fidelity toward materialism should inspire in him some distrust with respect to "this manner of conceiving the exterior world, tending to make it depend on the sole power of the Self and practically equivalent to negating it." [22] On the other hand, while surrealism developed, psychology was contesting the identification of image and sensation and subjecting it to severe criticism. With regard to normal perception, the old belief that images were taken for sensations was deemed wrong. For instance, the proofreader does not see, as real, images of the letters lacking in a word; Gestalt theory has dealt justly with the atomistic interpretation that so long allowed such a supposition. The word is not read by means of a previous perception of each of the details that, physically, constitute it; it is the object of a grasp confused and rectifiable but, from the very beginning, complete. Moreover, assuming that normal perception realizes the images it adds to the given, there is no proof that these images bring their strength with them. They may borrow it, as Hume already thought, from the liveliness of the sensations with which they are associated. As for the pathological state of psychosensorial hallucination, nobody anymore seems to claim that a simple image can gain there the plain and firm adhesion we encounter in actual perception. The image borrows its force from motor attitudes, from kinesthetic sensations provoked by changes in position of the sensorial organs, from delirium; so the hallucination remains poor, fixed, congealed, strange and foreign—it generally disappears in the doctor's presence; any systematic action seems to exclude it; its spatialization is uncertain; most often it has neither precision nor depth. It seems less present than distant, and there is room to believe that, appearing as it does in the sick who dream the world more than they perceive it, it testifies to the feebleness of their grasp on the real rather than the power of their images.

So the surrealists have been led to give to their belief in the realizing power of the imagination another significance. They seem often to search for the realizing force of imagination, not in the interior of the image, but in the synthesis in which the image is held, the synthesis that gives it its sense and seems the product of a desire. They prefer then, rather than a theory of hallucination and of detached images forcing themselves on us, the Freudian conception of dreams. This conception, too, admits that images invading consciousness might be taken for perceptions. But it explains their realization neither by their own power nor by the vague interpretation that they are capable of furnishing the sensations felt during sleep. These hypotheses, dear to Bergson, are abandoned. For Freud, in fact, the dream has a particular structure and a particular richness; it has sense and purposiveness. Guardian of sleep, it does not simply give the sensations we feel an arbitrary expression; it is in order to eliminate them as such that, when they menace the dream, it integrates them into its story, thus avoiding our waking up. Its incoherence is only apparent; we know how Freud, interpreting dreams—that is, restoring them —from their manifest content to the latent psychic process that they express, at their root discovered desire; taking into account, it goes without saying, the fact that this desire may be partial, condemned by use, and that the forces that in the waking state refuse it consciousness are still, in sleep, strong enough to impose a mask on it. Thus, the dream constitutes in itself alone a complete consciousness, distinct from the perceiving consciousness; the latter is regulated by the reality principle, the former by the pleasure principle.

Breton has often used the notions proposed in Freud's theory of dreams. Applying, in *Les Vases communicants*, a sort of psychoanalysis to the strange state of waking dream that, in the grip of despair, he came to live for several days, he employs the Freudian terms "condensation," "displacement," "substitution." [23] Some will protest no doubt that applying to a waking state the method instituted by Freud for dreams, Breton crosses the fundamental intent of psychoanalysis. Instead of wanting to situate oneiric or delirious thought in relation to rational thought, which is the aim of all psychiatry, does he not wish as a surrealist to break down the walls separating the two domains and make dream and waking appear as two "communicating vessels"? But we must not forget that Freud, in his *Psychopathology of Everyday Life,* likewise showed how our waking life bears traces of our unconscious desires and that Breton in his analysis of *Les Vases communicants,* though he discovers in normal perception and in dreams the same laws, never confuses the solidity of the psychic syntheses structured according to the reality principle with the fluidity of those swayed only by the pleasure principle. What he brings to light is that desire cuts "to shreds the stuff" of reality and to gain its ends uses while awake processes like those "it advances in order to realize itself while man sleeps." [24] This is why "the materials it uses" may be "real materials, things taken from life." Breton does not forget, thus, that the exterior world exists; he does not falter from his "confidence in it" and, when the rigidity of the real menaces him, is content to "extract from the environment, to the exclusion of all else," what must serve in the reconstitution of his self. He criticizes rather than approves the *pensée* of Pascal: "No one can be sure, without faith, if he wakes or if he sleeps." "What," he asks, "is this action brought against real life under pretext that sleep gives the illusion of this life?—an illusion discovered while waking, whereas in sleep real life, which must be sleep's illusion, is neither criticized nor taken for illusory." Finally, he explains the oneiric reconstruction of the world, pointing out that "everything becomes image and that the slightest object having been assigned no particular symbolic role is capable of representing no matter what." [25]

Obviously, the theory of imagination Breton advances here is not the one that led him in 1933 to glorify Teresa of Avila's vision of her wooden cross transformed into a crucifix of precious stones as "at once . . . imaginative and sensory," and to declare that "perception and representation—which seem to the ordinary adult radically opposed—are merely the dissociated products of a single, original faculty manifest in eidetic images and found to some extent in primitives and children," [26] and finally to remark that if psychoanalysis "has managed to charge some penetrable sense" into automatic improvisations, it is "far from casting light on the conditions under which a clearly valuable automatic text or drawing could be obtained." [27] This first conception, leading as we can see in several surrealist painters to letting internal images arise to trouble our perceptions, Dali rigorously adopts. Wanting to express internal perceptions visually, he is opposed to psychoanalysis and its interpretation of dream syntheses. "My whole ambition on the pictorial plane," Dali writes, "consists in materializing with the greatest imperialistic rage for precision images of concrete irrationality ... images which provisionally are neither explicable nor reducible by systems of logical intuition or by rational mechanisms. Images of concrete irrationality are thus images authentically unknown ... they are past the domain of psychoanalyzable phantasms and virtual representations." [28] Breton, on the contrary, never quite gives in to the irrationality of images. The control of lucidity and the moral norms of the significance of works always matter to him. He never gives up discovering the sense in any automatic production. To the riches of the unconscious he wishes to join the light of consciousness. This is why he prefers the Freudian conception—which searches for the strength of imaginative realization in a revealable desire and where ultimately madness is envisaged from the doctor's point of view (the psychoanalytic doctor who, instead of considering the products of madness from without, discovers their sense)—to the conception in which the force of realization seems to belong to the image itself, this retaining an absolute value and all its weight of mystery, madness being lived from the point of view of the patient who is its victim.

And no doubt it is not easy in surrealism to separate these two conceptions of imagination; they interpenetrate and are never clearly distinguished. Both in fact imply belief in the realizing power of imagination, the poet's necessity not to fake but to deliver himself "tied hand and foot" to its plans.[29] From whence surrealism, unlike Valery,[30] counting on "the torrential flow of automatic writing for the definitive cleaning of the literary stable" and wanting to "open wide the gates," [31] could not help noticing that the theory, according all reality to the image, is more entire, more decisive than that which sees in the image the product of some unconscious reason. This is why Breton never renounces it altogether and has some trouble answering the arguments of Dali, who when he declares that the paranoiac-critical activity considers images "in a coherent ensemble of systematic and significant relations" [32] seems to give Breton partial satisfaction. I believe, nevertheless, that in spirit the two conceptions of imagination that inspire surrealism are radically opposed, one being the expression of a sort of cosmological naturalism, the other a sort of humanism. If the image possesses in itself a power of realization, we must say that man is crossed by it; we find ourselves, in Herschel's words, in the presence of "a thought, an intelligence functioning in us but distinct from our personality." [33] It is here that Rimbaud's "I am thought" [34] would get all its force; like Leibniz's monad, man would realize, in each of his acts, a destiny conceived outside himself—of which he would be the involuntary expression. And we could join to this the idea of Novalis that, in Nelli's words, the form of a flower would be "of the same nature as the flora of our imagination," the "formative forces of plants" being analogous to the force that, for example, "makes us dream." But I cannot agree with Nelli that the essence of surrealism is conceiving the imaginary as "natural," "beyond the contradiction of materialism-idealism." [35] Breton could not be satisfied with a naturalistic romanticism in which human liberty would have ultimately no place. True, he does not abandon the idea of fate, which in a sense reduces liberty. But he can operate this reduction precisely because our fate is, for him as for Freud, the fruit of our profound tendencies, which are certainly volitional and, therefore, in some way free. Hence everything is changed. Our fate and the images that signify it continue, of course, to be imposed as if from without on our clear consciousness. They emanate none the less from a self formed of desires, and the "image" that is "my life" [36] expresses my profound personality and my individual spontaneity.

The surrealist imagination is not, then, reduced to a power that would extend the very force of Nature in us. Once more, surrealism, by the necessary development of

its share of Freudianism and of critical rationalism,
parts from romanticism. For romanticism, as Christian
Sénéchal remarks, "the dream is but one of numerous
states where the human soul, finding again its lost unity,
enters into communication with nature as a whole, therefore with divinity.... The soul ... is creative, because
it participates in the power of nature." For G. H. von
Schubert, nature "is the original of the world of dreams
... an embodied dream world." [37] And this naturalism
explains the romantics' retention, paradoxical at first
view, of a conception of imagination proceeding from the
Cartesians. For Descartes as for the romantics imagination is in effect nature erupting into our thought. The
Cartesians, it is true, and Spinoza himself, whose influence on the romantics was considerable, hold this intru-
sion of Nature into clear thought as a source of error;
truth is never acquired in their eyes except in the coherence of a reason first separated from worldly pursuits.
For the romantics, on the contrary, imagination is revelation. But opposed as they are in evaluating imagination,
the Cartesians, the romantics, and also, as we have seen,
Taine and Bergson agree on its nature. With Freud the
climate is totally different. Albert Béguin notes that between the romantic conception of the unconscious and
the Freudian theory there is "all the abyss separating a
mystical from a purely psychological doctrine." I think
we must go farther still and see that Freudianism, far
from remaining, as Béguin puts it, "in the purely ra-
tionalistic tradition," [38] is connected—in spite of its often
associationistic vocabulary—with the current of modern
thought that comes with phenomenology to deny the
image as such and to substitute for it the liberty and the
significant activity of an image-forming consciousness.
A humanistic conception, putting man at the center of
things and at the basis of his own thoughts, here replaces a cosmological and pantheistic vision. How deny
that surrealism participates to the highest degree in this
new spirit, when imagination becomes for it—even more

than realizing force—power of refusal, of derealization, of selection, of choice, of significance, and of comprehension? The surrealist imagination refuses the given and derealizes it; desire chooses whatever in ordinary life pleases it, and, the logical boundaries of perception being broken, all approaches become permissible and all are sources of light. Can one conceive such an imagination apart from human consciousness, and without recognizing that for the surrealists Freud has played the role of Kant, conducting them in a sort of new Copernican revolution, to explain subjectively what they had first believed simply a product of Nature? Thus, more and more surrealism turns from the psychological to the poetic sense of the word image; it replaces representational images with comparative images and, like Reverdy, it assumes that "the spirit alone" seizes the relations that constitute it.[39] "The spirit," Breton says in this connection, "is marvelously prompt in seizing the most feeble relation that may exist between two objects taken at random"; the slightest object "is capable of representing no matter what." "Comparing two objects as distant as possible from each other or putting them together by any other method in an abrupt and startling manner remains the highest task to which poetry can aspire. In this its unequaled and unique power must tend more and more to be exercised..."[40] Here it cannot be doubted we are no longer in a philosophy of Nature but in a philosophy of Spirit, of language, and of freedom. Doubtless, this Spirit, this language, this freedom are not measured by our clear consciousness. The conscious and the unconscious are equally expressed; desire retains an essential place; thought seems sometimes even collective or universal. But this thought has all the character of human thought. It is related to the reflection that enables us to free ourselves from the given, taking in relation to it that step backward which is the sign of our autonomy. It chooses, it comprehends, it invents. It is not the road leading from the image to the real, the blind natural force by which forms are incarnated. It is much rather the liberating faculty that permits us to pass from the real to the image itself.

ii. The Imaginary and Beauty

It is not easy to give rationalism its due. In introducing into its conception of imagination an element of critical consciousness, will surrealism not be constrained to renounce its fundamental project and to justify scientific and technological activity as the only way—at the level of objective knowledge—that the imaginary can become real? If the image is born from our rupture with spontaneous and vital adaptation, from the step back that we can take in relation to immediate engagement, we can no longer in effect find the real through the image except by acknowledging still more our first separation from nature and submitting our desire to the laws of our representation. On the level of pure spontaneity and instinct, we can conceive of an action directly extending the affections. But precisely on this level, there are no images properly so called. Dolorific, tactile, olfactory, and gustatory sensations, which express the animal nature in us, are not images, cannot even be recalled in the form of images and hence are not sources of reflective behavior. Here the object is up against us, practically joined to our body; we cannot distance it. From whence the still affective and living aspect of the reactions that follow: abrupt withdrawal of the hand, intake of breath, nausea. Properly human actions are, on the contrary, linked to the development of auditory and visual sensations. These sensations are easily extended into images and this, as Pradines has shown, is because they are already images. Pradines, studying the differentiation which can bring a properly representative sensibility out of a primitive, affective one, establishes that representation is possible in effect in proportion as the objects presented to our auditory or visual sensations remain at some distance. Our adaptation to the situation they signify can thus lose any corporeal urgency. Indeed, often the heard or seen world does not interest our needs, or at least does not concern our affective interests. If then—while dolorific or tactile or olfactory or gustatory images are rare and vague—there are many visual and auditory images, recalling absent objects with precision, it is because the visual and auditory sensations, more or less nonaffective, already signify distance and hence the absence of the represented objects. The image appears, even in the sensation, in company with play, with distance, with the possibility for the subject to separate himself from his perception and to make it into spectacle. And scientific knowledge and reflective action derive from the image. Separating the object from the actual synthesis where it was experienced puts us in a position to discover objective laws, which are nothing else than the structure of this representation itself. Acoustics and optics are born when man, ceasing to aspire to things by way of their qualities, as animals do, first isolated sounds and colors in their capacity of images. And the science of the laws of objects in its turn renders possible technological action, the indirect realization of human desire by observation of the relations that reason has discovered and by submission of our impatience to the laws of physics.

Now if this is so, the appearance of the image, which seemed to us at first provider and nourisher of the surrealist hope, comes on the contrary to mark the end of that "life of presence" [41] that surrealism has always wished to recover. And this spirit, whose liberty instead of extending the natural and vital attitude inverts it in order to arrive at representation, is revealed as the very thing surrealism has ceaselessly indicted. In the world of science and of technological enterprise where its processes are introduced, how would forms tending to be realized find a place? How would the poem "Tournesol" ten years later be incarnated in that "night of the sunflower" so essential to the fate of Breton? [42] From now on the separation that bears images will always make its despairing split felt; the imaginary, far from being penetrated by the heat of desire, will be illuminated only by the light of reason. It is through with any "thrill," any emotion even, any of the knowledge that is love. From there, can we, as Breton hoped, "gain a consciousness at once still clearer and still more impassioned of the sensible world," [43] or even, as Jean Brun asks, maintain that sensation is "more than a magical marriage" and both comprehends and goes beyond "the throbbing psychological mechanism that presided at its birth?" [44] Quite the contrary, we seem to have renounced, once for all, in constructing the image, the affective grip on things that alone can maintain a direct contact with their being. Here we have lost even the medieval nature, in continuity with being and with man, whose secrets the alchemists tried to recover. Technological science does not make things as Nature makes them; born of the constitution of the object by the rupture with ontology, it can no longer find the real except by the paths of reason. Everything here is language, and language will never be able altogether to turn against language to let appear what it only expresses symbolically. All is vision, and who cannot see that vision is possible only at a distance? The very essence of the human glance introduces some separation into visual knowledge.

And no doubt the progress of our perception, making qualities appear as such, is also the source of artistic vision and audition. Pradines remarks in this connection that the representative sensibility, after differentiating from the primitive sensibility, divides in its turn, producing a sort of secondary affectivity, of properly aesthetic sensibility. The senses of sight and hearing, naturally nonaffective, can then give place to pleasures of a new order, independent of the satisfaction of needs and proper to mankind; a pure color or sound capable of inspiring in us a veritable ecstasy.[45] In this a kind of emotion is born that will attain its full richness when provoked, not by a simple sensory element, but by relations of lines, colors, sounds, relations contemplated by us disinterestedly, detached from all practical utility and all realistic aims. Who cannot see, however, that with such an aesthetics we are on the trail of a formal beauty, the beauty-as-spectacle that surrealism has always condemned? Surrealism, while the enemy of a flatly realistic art, is not, for all that, partisan of a formal and nonrepresentational art. It does not judge works according to some golden section. Surrealist paintings are not symphonies of colors and forms. Certainly, surrealism is always very attentive to the quality of expression and professes that "subjective emotion, whatever its intensity, is not directly creative in art." [46] But it does not consider that to render emotion creative it is enough to organize one's expression by calculation; one must, on the contrary, restore it "to this living hearth from whence alone it can radiate," [47] a hearth that can be discovered only by returning to that original faculty, "traces of which remain among primitives and children" and which "lift the curse of an uncrossable barrier between interior and exterior worlds." To regain this faculty, Breton thinks, "would be man's salvation." [48] "A work can be taken as surrealist only inasmuch as the artist has tried to attain the total psychophysical field (of which the field of consciousness is only a small part)." [49] Does not all this indicate that the true vocation of surrealism must lead it to renounce whatever in imagination is separation, distance, analysis, and recoil? Can surrealism legitimately go beyond the automatism that, evading all reflection and any free project, lets a purely natural activity be expressed in us?

I think it can, and that once again it is by assuming an apparent contradiction that surrealism reveals the profundity of its project and its fidelity to man. The difficulty in this is analogous to what Bergson encountered when, intuiting that animal instinct held the secret of

life, he became aware that instinct is ignorant of the
secret, because it is unconscious. Thus, the revelation of
the secret could be attained only through a mysterious
illumination of instinct by intelligence itself. In surrealism we likewise see clear knowledge go in search of what
is within, preparing to welcome it; what is within comes
meanwhile to trouble our clear positive vision. But whatever the route traveled, whether from the real to the
imaginary or from the imaginary to the real, it remains
that illumination presupposes the two realms in rapport
and is born from their encounter. Certainly, the surrealists always evoke with regret the primal fusion that is
taken from us by our objective vision of the world.
They are not satisfied with alienation, with the mutilation assumed by technological science; they praise childhood because its "absence of all known rigor ... permits
the perspective of many lives led at once." [50] But they
do not wish to go back into night. They want the forces
of night manifest in daylight, first of all that they might
trouble a day forgetful of those forces. The phantoms
that surrealism hopes to bring back cannot be seen by us
and cannot be manifested as forces of night except by
the effect of some day casting light on them. In fact the
phantom that Chirico, Aragon, and Breton saw one day
in the Place Pigalle had the look "of a child come to sell
flowers." [51]

We know with what insistence Breton has come back
to the idea of a "unique, original faculty" of which
"physical perception and mental representation" would
be "the products of its dissociation." [52] Can Breton believe, however, that this faculty has existed in the capacity of a self-conscious faculty? Can he desire a positive return to a past state of man, or of humanity? I
think, on the contrary, that the originality of his position
is in the apparent indetermination that it assumes toward
real duration, an indetermination that forbids our deciding whether the sentiment is one of regret, of historical
expectation, or of hope in the present. What in any case

seems certain is that the relation of the surrealist state and immediates like the unconscious, dreams, and pure enjoyment is always a relation with a remainder of exteriority, a relation of partial belonging where the immediate is desired rather than attained and—using Descartes' vocabulary—touched rather than comprehended. Surrealism is semirevelation, or if you prefer, revelation of a night into which one may not altogether enter, in the midst of a day whose brightness cannot satisfy us either and which, besides, would lose its sense of day if it ceased to light up objects whose being is not light but opacity. The surrealist consciousness is thus, above all, "relation" and is always born at the birth of a relation. In the majority of surrealist texts, the dream crops out, but it is moving only to the extent that we do not deliver ourselves entirely to it; it is only by its contact with the verities of reason—that which it troubles and by which it is illuminated—that the dream seems marvelous. So Benjamin Péret does not hesitate to give his characters true logical anxieties and to introduce into his most distracting narratives the most exact details. "His emotion was intense; would he go at the first stroke to accomplish his aim and would he learn from the singular person who dumped his bath out the window why summer follows spring? In the time it took to drop a tear for his sister who died last year, he knocked at the door indicated to him. The cry of a cock resounded followed almost immediately by a panicked bleating ... A third time he rapped on the door, but this time the silence was complete. He was perplexed; but still, if a bath had fallen at his feet, someone must have thrown it? ... The flame of a torch allowed him to see the room he had gotten into. A verdant stretch of lawn, well watered and clipped, occupied it." [53] The use of words in false senses, or at least in usages hard at first to grasp and necessitating explanatory notes (such as, "to be employed for the black: to be leaves giving shade," "to play the sap: to run away," "strawberries: large drops of rain," "burner:

the sun," "hat: sky"),[54] arrive at the same result: language here is on the surface of dream and becomes similar to talking to oneself when one is terribly fatigued. And we know how the data of automatism most often flows for the surrealists in a correct and coherent syntax; consciousness and reason collaborate with chance and the unconscious. In the same way surrealist painting destroys the visible object but, since it remains something unseen, reminds us of the laws of vision. Surrealism then does not present itself as a return to the immediate, but as a contact with the immediate, which is completely different. This contact may take the form of expectation, expectation being something only those who do not possess what they hope for can feel. It sometimes becomes nostalgia, nostalgia inhabiting those who are not efficient in returning to what they long for. Further yet, it is the essence of poetry, and it is then in the present that this semibelonging is experienced, this instantaneous promise of we-do-not-know-what. Dream mingles with waking life, the affective consciousness with the intellectual. Spirit enters into rapport with the Other, and this is why it is love.

So the apparent obscurities of surrealism are explained. We have seen how it is tempted by sadism. But the temptation to sadism is no more sadism than pure enjoyment is love. Enjoyment negates the Other, or forgets him; love is recognition of the Other as other, and I have always thought in this connection how if Breton was unable to love Nadja, it is because she was not "the other" for him but was surrealism itself, with which he coincided. For Nadja, on the other hand, Breton was the Other in that he was reason. And likewise, imagination of the sadistic act is not a sadistic act; it is self-knowledge, and hence surpassing what is sadistic in us by a lucidity that, in order to know, must be partly detached. The enticement of dream is not the dream; it is augmentation of consciousness in a being for whom day to day positivism endangers the sense of the marvelous. And I think it is thus that we must understand the total recuperation of human powers that Breton proclaims. "Let us remember," he says, "that the idea of surrealism tends simply to the total recuperation of our psychic strength by a means that is simply the vertiginous descent into ourselves, the systematic illumination of hidden places and the progressive darkening of other places, perpetual promenading right in the middle of forbidden zones." [55] The "progressive darkening of other places" seems to me to be added simply for the quality of the image and to express revolt against the tyranny of objectivity; the battle against the censure that hinders us from knowing ourselves will never be waged to the full unless we decide to attack it, not only in its moral structure, but also in its alliance with a reality principle the plainest effect of which is keeping subjective and objective from rejoining. It is in destroying the logical solidity of objects that surrealism will be able to find again all that we are. But finding what we are is not losing consciousness; it is augmenting our consciousness. And our consciousness grows only by ever new relatings. These keep man from being limited, from being alienated in a partial activity. Does he conceive the world only on the level of the scientific object? Surrealism recalls the rights of the marvelous. Is he lost in work? Surrealism tells him of pleasure, of ravishment. To every too rapid synthesis surrealism opposes the procedures of disintegration. But when spirit is lost, surrealism returns to integration and synthesis. It recommends that we give ourselves over to automatism, then counsels us to become double and to take consciousness of what is happening in us when we write. So proceeds this "systematic illumination," an incessant combat against limitation and oblivion. Anxious to recover the totality of our powers, in love with being and not with the void, surrealism wishes to liberate thought of any order that tends to become normative. It recalls that thought is the source of all order. But it does not allow thought to disappear in a nocturnal experience that would be pure fusion with what is within. Rather, it wishes, with psychoanalysis, to find the sense of what is within, along with whatever is on the margins of consciousness.

Surrealism's attitude toward the beyond is permeated by the same reserve. It welcomes promise, not the illusion of possession. Doubt always enters to save lucidity and the freedom of the spirit giving judgment; and so surrealism shows itself faithful to one of the first affirmations of Breton: "The single word liberty is all that still excites me." [56] For the free spirit cannot be entirely confounded with what it is not; it cannot mistake its belief for knowledge. Hence the objective chance is no longer recognized except as "index of possible reconciliation between the aims of nature and the aims of mankind, in the view of the latter." [57] The encounter of subjectivity and objectivity is interpreted in the realm of the marvelous; the synthesis of present and future operates in the imaginary; poetry no longer refuses to be elevated to pure essence. Recording with approval that poetry had never "been as widely appreciated" as during the war, Breton adds: "It is easy to recognize in this phenomenon the manifestation of the necessity for a *detour by way of essence* such as one feels whenever individual existence or even the pursuit of any particular chance within the framework of that existence is imperiled." [58] The Platonic tone of this affirmation is unmistakable. For in such a climate, hope and expectation and nostalgia necessarily take on the form of the unique beauty and can be experienced only in the grip of an emotion that we must call aesthetic. It is in this sense that the surrealist conception of beauty cannot altogether be separated from the Platonic theory or even from the analyses of Kant concerning aesthetic and teleological judgment. Like Plato, Breton sees in beauty the annunciation of some return, of some ontological discovery, of some reconciliation. But the Being thus approached is never actually seized, and this is where the surrealist affirmation is faithful to the Kantian reflection, which marvels at an appearance of purposiveness but will not affirm its reality. In beauty as Kant conceives it there is a foreboding of ontology that does not attain to ontology. "All art and all nature," Gaëtan Picon writes in this regard, "to the extent they give us an aesthetic impression, appear if not as a direct revelation of the supersensible at least as an allusion to it, if not as a guarantee at least as a positing of the absolute." [59] This positing of the absolute we have run onto many times in surrealism. But the surrealist revelation never, properly speaking, pretends to knowledge. Surrealism never quite espouses the idea that aesthetic emotion implies a knowledge superior to scientific knowledge. Rather than knowing, art is for them a ground of valuing. No doubt human consciousness passes quickly from valuing to affirming theoretically—so our adherence to dream is explained, so madness is born where the affirmation of values desired by the patient, and necessary to his life, lead him to believe in a world in which such values would be realized. But surrealism, though it uses dream and madness, does not succumb. Its adherence to the imaginary is never complete, or rather consciousness accepts that for what it is worth and not for a grasp of reality. The imaginary thus appears beautiful, and in its hold beauty is recognized as beauty. Surrealist beauty is the imaginary itself, refusing to be related to anything but itself or to go beyond itself toward an aim that would transcend it.

Emile Bouvier has remarked that "the notion of pure literary beauty dominates . . . all contemporary research." "The emotional shock of pure literary beauty," he writes, "is sufficient unto itself. And this criterion of perfection will replace the old intellectual standards: fidelity of reproduction or rational adherence. Beauty will no longer be the equation of the work to its object, but its capacity in pure literary emotions." [60] Bouvier here calls "literary" what the surrealists call "poetic." The surrealists in fact reject, under the label "literary," beauty-as-expression and beauty-as-spectacle. There is no conscious and calculated expression with them, since the poet, listening to a language of whose sense he himself is ignorant, is continually excelled by what he reveals. No contemplated and detached spectacle of life: the inwardness of our unconscious desires comes to trouble the designs of our reason, and hope in the reconciliation of subjective and objective brings into play the destiny of man as a whole. In the eyes of the surrealists, beauty-as-spectacle—ignorant of death and giving no solution to man's problems—received a mortal blow during the crisis of consciousness following the war. Breton calls a beauty that can contain all man's problems and all his distresses a beauty "convulsive," "veiled-erotic," "fixed-exploding," "circumstantial-magical." [61] There can be no doubt that here art proposes itself new aims, is charged with an infinite hope, becomes with love the unique messenger of man's expectation. But beauty, as Bouvier remarks, cannot properly be surpassed, leaves no place for knowledge. Its domain is hope, not possession; analogy, not identity. The mysterious links between things are discovered only in the form of symbols. Beauty becomes pure beauty, not in being separated from the world, but because all the problems of the world lead man there and seem to be contained there—and in such a way that beauty cannot refer to anything superior to itself, or at least cannot state in rational discourse to what it refers. Such a beauty is not interpretable. It is not a solution, but it is the question that human knowledge cannot get past. It is the last form of hope for those who will not affirm more than they know. It is the proof that in the most tragic circumstances something appears and gleams which condemns despair. Thus, writes Breton, "the work of Watteau has . . . the good fortune of making us conjure all that could be appalling in considering the egotism and meanness of men in periods of reverse into its sole glory. . . . We are more and more brought to see that whole atrocious epoch through his dream. When he touches the apparel of the soldiers of his time, those three-cornered hats, the coattails, the leather, he sings only what shines in the eyes of the girls and makes them show off the suppleness of their figures, the spring of their bosoms.... Thus any tempest, the first good day around, finds means to be swallowed and negated in a pearl." [62] There we have salvation by art, which is assuredly not salvation by literature, but by beauty. Here mysticism, religious dogmatism, Gerard de Nerval's madness in believing he could converse "with the choir of stars taking part" in his joys and his sorrows,[63] find their just measure and their success in man. For man may and must go beyond anything in which he is lost, limited, alienated. Only he cannot go beyond man.

iii. The Imaginary and the Surreal

In Hegel's system, Art is the immediate moment of the absolute Spirit. It is surpassed only by revealed Religion and by Philosophy. Breton does not believe in Religion and judges the Absolute Knowledge impossible. He holds, therefore, with Art. But Art is then charged with all the responsibilities of Religion and Philosophy. Of course, it will always be easy to claim that surrealism, expressing itself with words, is a literary art. It seeks to take language at its source and lead it to its blossoming; it prefers verbal messages to visual images. Writing, even if automatic, remains none the less writing. But it is enough to compare, for example, the rhetorical and grammatical preoccupations of Valéry and the concerns of Breton to gage the difference. "A greater emancipation of spirit and not a greater formal perfection must remain the principal objective," writes Breton; the works he says he is interested in at the moment are those of Raymond Abellio, Malcolm de Chazal, Jean-Louis Bouquet, André Pieyre de Mandiargues, Maurice Raphaël, and Paroutaud. And what he looks for in them is "penetration of the world by the occult way," "the detection of a new fantasy," "lyric cryptesthesia of the lower depths," and "apprehension of the future." [64] Breton wants to promote an ethic whose essential rule would be, "To each according to his desires." [65] He proposes to modify the social condition, he is attentive to the human condition. If he is attached to language, it is to identify it with man, to make of it, as Maurice Blanchot put it, "human liberty acting and manifesting." [66] Searching for a way of salvation, he questions himself about the unusual, on the privileged moments of exaltation and of illumination; he begins listening to dreams. He wants to rebuild love.[67] The fundamental project of Breton—affirmed since 1924 and, despite its appearance in various guises, never altered— is not essentially literary. And if he seems to end up with the single consideration of beauty, it is because the consciousness of beauty is today the one which most adequately permits grasping man's authenticity. Since modern man has lost religious faith and metaphysical comprehension, he is led to make a life out of art, to ask of beauty the sense of his destiny. Art, no longer outshone by religion and philosophic knowledge, as it was for Hegel, seems like the supreme moment of the spirit.

All consciousness, however, aims at an object and is defined by what it is conscious of. What in surrealism, then, is the correlative of the aesthetic consciousness? To declare that it is beauty is, no doubt, to say nothing, to forge a pseudo-object, to double the aesthetic consciousness uselessly with its own reflection. It is in this sense that Breton replies to André Parinaud that "artists, not only the modern poets, do not necessarily look for beauty," [68] and that he always maintains the absolutely subjective character of the aesthetic consciousness. Everything in art, he writes, depends on the liberty with which imagination "manages to put itself on the stage and to put only itself on the stage." [69] According to Breton, modern painting rejoins poetry in this direction and considers "nature only in its rapport with the interior world of consciousness." It is "followed in this by sculpture, as the experience of Giacometti and Arp testifies." [70] Now an art that submits no longer to the criterion of the exterior object can no longer be considered as aiming at a beauty-object, a beauty objectively definable. [71] How should we attain to such a beauty if we must distinguish it both from the physical object in which it is incarnated and from the emotion in which it is revealed? It is clear, on the contrary, that beauty as such is confused with the feeling of the beautiful and that we cannot talk of a consciousness of beauty in the sense that we speak of consciousness of an objective reality. Beauty is not distinct from the consciousness we take of it. It is a manner of taking consciousness of things. If it is not confused with the individuality of a taste, its universality remains, as Kant saw, that of a subjective disposition; it arises from an accord, a harmony between the faculties common to all men. Would one like to part from this subjectivity and consider that beauty leads to truth or to the Good? He must then, as Plato did, give as correlative to the consciousness of the Beautiful a world of Ideas whose reality is not itself aesthetic and suppose that our aesthetic emotion expresses the souvenir or presentiment of that world. Surrealism refuses this step. The surrealist consciousness does not pose as consciousness of a conceptual verity or a transcendent moral value, any more than it refers to objective beauty. Once more, then, what is the correlative of this ravished, attentive, unquiet consciousness, of this religious consciousness no longer oriented toward any dogmatic or revealed contents, this metaphysical consciousness that no longer believes in metaphysics? Its correlative is the surreal, and this is why we may say that the surreal is the aim of the surrealist consciousness. It is to this consciousness what physical objectivity is to the scientific consciousness, what Being—whose function it often fulfills—is to the metaphysical consciousness. And it is in this sense that I have sometimes likened the surrealist approach to the Platonic. But it remains very difficult to define the surreal, if the consciousness to which it corresponds refuses to be contemplative and must conserve the liberty, the availability that, for the surrealists, cannot be lost without losing man, and without which we always fall into some alienation. All the apparent hesitations of surrealism derive, without any doubt, from this difficulty. If, in effect, in order to define surreality we aim at the surreal itself, we shall be brought to transforming it into an object, speaking of it as of a thing. We shall no longer avoid a religious or hermetic dogmatism. If, on the contrary, we attempt to describe and study consciousness of the surreal, we shall not get past psychologism; then we shall make consciousness itself into an object, treating it as psychiatrists treat madmen or as anthropologists treat primitives. The richness, the sense, the power of revelation inherent in the surrealist consciousness will be lost.

Surrealism has always determined to avoid this double danger, and this is why we can not reduce it either to an objectivism or to a subjectivism. In 1924 Breton defined surreality as "a sort of absolute reality." [72] But the absolute is precisely what we cannot speak of without rendering it relative to language. In speaking of the absolute we necessarily fall back into some religion, and no doubt it was from experiences like those surrealism invokes that religions were formed—by giving as correlative to the consciousness that lived these experiences an affirmed and determined dogma or, more simply, some definable truth on the level of objects, which from then on it was necessary to believe in. Thus, the Other toward which man's consciousness is essentially directed is forever reduced to language; it becomes another world. Surrealism wishes to conserve the essence of the religious consciousness, refusing what it considers alienation. It admits and recognizes all human aspiration and Pascal's attitude seems to it "among the most justifiable on the emotional level." [73] But it refuses all dogma, all formulated content, all discourse properly cosmological. For reasons already seen, Breton can never thoroughly adopt the vision of the real that occultists or hermeticists pro-

pose for us. Does he accept even the primitive consciousness he so often discusses? Certainly, as Monnerot remarks, "the surreal or marvelous that the surrealists are
aiming at suggests without too much abuse of language
the real-imaginary world of certain primitives, and anal-
ogies between what the latter live and what the former
look for are striking." [74] But still, "live" and "look for"
presuppose very different attitudes. While for primitives
"there is no split between the surreal and ordinary life,
but continuity . . ." "the surrealist rarely invokes the possible experience of the surreal except against everyday
life and the social boundaries that contain it and determine it and tolerate nothing outside it." [75] The unusual
is for the primitive "more often baneful than propiti-
ous"; [76] for Breton it awakens hope. Thus, we must conclude that the surrealist consciousness is no more primitive than it is religious; the surrealist appeal to primitive
consciousness hardly allows discovery except of ourselves. For, once more, it is one thing to be at the stage
of immediate consciousness and another to wish to return, to feel nostalgia, to suppose that "man, originally in
possession of certain keys which held him in close com-
munion with nature, lost them and since then more and
more feverishly persists in trying others that do not
work." [77] In surrealism the appeal to the primitive consciousness is always a function of what the modern consciousness has become. It is a question of disalienating a
spirit lost in the single consideration of objective reality
and making of scientific and technological experience,
which is but one of its possible experiences, the measure
of all reality. So the surreal, which for the primitive is
confused with the objective real, appears here as what
derealizes an everyday real—to which, however, it remains immanent.

But surrealism objects even more to making the primitive or dreaming or delirious consciousness into an object
of study, a thing. It knows that we cannot comprehend a
consciousness except by remaining faithful to its aims.

It tries, therefore, continuing to question itself on the value of its revelations, to find again that first experience from which are born myths, religions, credos. Since the *Manifesto*, Breton refuses to restore dreams "to a parenthesis," distinguishes the sum of their moments from the sum of his "moments of waking," asks himself if last night's dream does not follow "that of the preceding night," and is uneasy to know whether the confusion we feel in the presence of certain women might not have its source in what connects these women with our dreams. He wants to discover "the key to this corridor," [78] and nothing better indicates his preoccupation than the constant return, in his work, of the word "key." Thus, the characters put on stage at the beginning of *L'Amour fou* hold "the keys to the situations," [79] and Breton relies on desire as on a "tall turnkey." [80] Dreams and the tendencies they express, the deepest of which—as psychoanalysis has shown—construct our fate, are ceaselessly interrogated by surrealism. There is no question here of evasion, still less of fantasy; it is a question of finding the sense of our existence, of clarifying our destiny by discovering a principle of order and coordination distinct from reason. Later, Breton enlarges his enquiry: he extends it to madness, to the mythical consciousness, to the excitement of encounters. Persuaded "that the fate of human communities is assessed by variations in the power their conditioning myths retain over them," attributing to the absence of such myths the collapse of "the France of 1939–1940, whose official representatives had engaged it so long in a sceptical and blasé path," [81] he accords to the mythical consciousness a value of contact with the surreality from which, more or less obscurely, he expects man's salvation. Instead of asking psychologically, as do so many moderns since Benjamin Constant, if he does or does not love, Breton searches metaphysically for what love means. In him everything is movement toward some other thing, appeal, waiting for a signal. And all the surrealists participate in this quest. Victor Brauner declares himself "emperor of the realm of personal myth." [82] Aragon recognizes that the peculiarity of the evolution of his thought is "a mechanism in every point analogous to the genesis of myths"; "man," according to him, "is full of gods, like a sponge immersed in deep sky." [83] He condemns psychology, which leads us "to forget the abyss and the torments of the infinite." [84] He attempts to communicate with "the divined divinity," [85] haunts what he calls "holy places," [86] perceives everywhere—even in "the red and white squares of the tablecloth"—"the unknowable showing through," [87] hears in the most banal phrases "mad words speaking of happiness." [88] And no doubt Aragon always mixes with his search for the surreal some outrage, some provocation and also some irony, some humoristic or depreciatory whim that makes the exact evaluation of his true intention difficult.[89] *Le Paysan de Paris,* even more than an appeal to the surreal, presents itself as a critique of the surreal by its reduction to love: "Am I going to pursue," Aragon asks, ". . . this lying description of a park which three friends one day entered? What's the use: you have risen over this park, over the people strolling, over thought. Your outline and your perfume, they are what possess me." [90] But Aragon seems to interpret love itself metaphysically, which brings us back to some surreality: "Now ready to believe everything, flowers could spring at her steps, she would make broad daylight of the night, and all the phantasmagorias of drunkenness and of imagination would be nothing extraordinary. If they do not love, it is because they are ignorant." [91] In this, love is not considered as a state felt but as an "overture toward," and thus as consciousness. We find again the movement that permits Eluard to write:

> *And I so love you I no longer know*
> *Which of us is absent* [92]

which makes Georges Hugnet say:

> *all her gestures attract lights and gather in* [93]

and permits Breton to see in woman a résumé of the
mysteries of Nature and in love an introduction to the
knowledge of all the realities in Nature:

> *My wife with hair of wood fire*
> *With thoughts of heat-lightning*
> *With figure of hour-glass*
>
> . . . .
>
> *My wife with temples of slate from greenhouse roof*
> *And steam on the panes*
> *My wife with shoulders of champagne*
> *And of fountain with dolphins' heads under ice*
>
> . . . .
>
> *My wife with armpits of marten and beechnuts*
> *Of Midsummernight*
>
> . . . .
>
> *My wife with calves of pith of elder*
>
> . . . .
>
> *My wife with neck of unpearled barley*
> *My wife with throat of Valley of Gold*
> *Of rendezvous in the very bed of the torrent*
> *With breasts of night*
>
> . . . .
>
> *My wife with sex of seaweed and old candies*
>
> . . . .
>
> *My wife with eyes of savannah*
> . . . . . . [94]

Thus, the poetic state is never, for the surrealists,
treated as a state; it is lived and thought as interrogation,
as question, as direction, as semidiscovery and, in Monnerot's phrase, "groping-toward." [95] This is how the surrealists, often desirous of allowing subjectivity to invade
objectivity and master it, nevertheless steer clear of psychologism. They never neglect the intentional character
of consciousness; the self never closes on itself and makes
do, in a sort of blind egoism, with enjoyment or pleasure.
Obsessed by a "floor whose grooves a thousand washings

had accentuated," Max Ernst decided "to interrogate the symbolism of this obsession." He then took "a series of drawings from the planks, by dropping sheets of paper on them at random," then "rubbing them with a lead pencil." He thus invented a procedure of rubbing, by which he intensified "the irritability of the spiritual faculties" and interrogated "all sorts of materials ... leaves and their veins, the frayed edges of a cloth bag," before uniting the results in his *Histoire naturelle*.[96] And we know the importance that surrealism has always attached to the counsel of Leonardo da Vinci, commanding "his students who looked for an original and suitable subject to gaze a long time at an old ruined wall. It will not be long, he told them, before you begin to see little by little forms and scenes becoming more and more precise." [97] In all this the same attempt is expressed, the same organization of "perceptions with objective tendency," calling "imperiously, in external reality, something that replies to them," [98] the same will to discovery and deciphering. For every object, even in the open, seems at first to hide its true reality from us; it is revealed only by our uneasy attention. This is what is expressed in Magritte's composition, which presents to our view a too visible naked woman, and around her the words: "I do not see the ... hidden in the forest." [99] Breton writes:

> The stream in this very curl as in no other among all
>   streams
> Is master of a secret it cannot make ours in flight
>
> .   .   .   .
>
> But nothing is verified all are afraid ourselves
> Are almost afraid too
> And still I am sure that behind the locked woods that
>   turn in this moment against the pane
> The only clearing opens ...[100]

We see to what point Breton carries seriously the poetic consciousness of expectation, of annunciation; each perception appears first as a sort of void that sur-

reality will fill halfway. And yet the concern to distinguish poetic analogy from mystical analogy always constrains Breton to declare that poetic analogy is "all
empirical" and "never presupposes, across the woof of
the visible world, an invisible universe tending to be
manifested." [101] The surreal, then, is not the supernatural,
and this is why, despite the metaphysical uneasiness of
the surrealist consciousness, it cannot be considered as
the correlative of a religious or mystical consciousness,
but only of an artistic one. And, of course, the conception the surrealists hold of art, where its emancipating
power is never forgotten, renders this consciousness indissolubly aesthetic and moral. The analogical image, Breton
maintains, "moves, between the two present realities, in
a determined direction which is irreversible. From the
first of these realities to the second it marks a vital tension turned to the utmost toward health, pleasure, quie-
tude, grace rendered, accepted use. It has for mortal
enemies the depreciatory and the depressing." [102] But we
see that the state felt by man, and not the envisaged goal,
is here again the unique criterion. Breton declares that
the exigency he brings to light "could well be of an
ethical order," but fearing to turn the surrealist conquests
"to the glory of some sort of beyond," he will not have it
taken as metaphysics. So that once again hope does not
know what it is expectation of; the will not to go beyond
man, which forbade surrealism to prefer the loved one
over love or the object of desire over desire, now obliges
it to be content with beauty—which at first was only a
promise—and to see in beauty "the great refuge." [103]
Surrealism has often been reproached for its outrages.
For my part, I am struck rather by its excess of prudence
in the ontological affirmation. Always on the path of
Platonism and metaphysics, it doubts the world of Ideas
and denies God. If sometimes, lacking the loved being,
Breton passes "from being to essence," and takes from
"the collective person of woman" "the idea that all is not
lost," it is always as makeshift and "the spirit's second-

best for the possibility of return to being"—always to be understood, of course, as a particular being.[104] And tempted by occultism, if not by religion, surrealism remains on the borderline of belief and refuses any precise formulation of a faith. It seems, moreover, not to know what the word faith means, and, understanding perfectly well that the reality expressed by religions and myths cannot be known literally, it seems incapable of deciding whether they can or cannot be believed in. Opposed to all objective systems in the name of hope, and careful not to give hope a content that would put us back on the level of objects, it even refuses to accord a metaphysical sense to its aspiration.

In that way, and while respecting the intentional character of consciousness, surrealism reduces man to himself and rejects everything that transcends him. Not that it makes man into a God, as Carrouges thinks, or even a superman. I have trouble agreeing with Gabriel Rey that surrealism is a "superhumanism" born from romanticism.[105] Breton always remembers that man is mortal; he recalls, with Pascal, that "his greatness is one with his misery;" he does not forget "the flagrant disproportion between the breadth of man's aspirations and the individual limits of his life." [106] But we can ask then whether surrealist humanism does not contain, despite its fundamental project, profound reasons for despair. Maurice Nadeau and Guy Dupré have spoken of surrealist pessimism.[107] Does ravishment before the marvelous, which constitutes the climate of surrealism, suffice to distinguish it philosophically from the existentialist humanism which today has so widely taken its place? Not preferring what it hopes for to hoping, what it desires to desiring, what it loves to loving, refusing on the other hand that sort of blind epicureanism of enjoying hope and desire and love as states void of meaning—does this not necessarily lead us to the existentialist theme of anguish and to a consciousness opening onto nothingness? Detached from any transcendence and any vertical dimension, is not surrealist liberty—mistress of an enchanted world on which she confers in turn the most troubling and the most promising senses—the same as existentialist liberty, whose last word is to merge with the surrounding situation? Truly, the purely humanistic consciousness, the consciousness desirous of recognizing nothing outside man, never quite knows whether the spark that impels it toward life is of hope or of despair. To say that man is all, is this not to say that he finds around him nothing but void? Certainly, surrealism represents in the history of humanism the most daring and most total project ever conceived to render to man all his rights to happiness and the free use of his passions. But can one save man without recourse to anything beyond man? Will the surreal give us a reason for living if it will not put itself more clearly on the side of transcendence, at the risk of approaching the supernatural? And would not surrealism, rightly discrediting any beyond verbally, and thus objectively, qualified, have to substitute a surreal retaining at least its ontological weight? There is some paradox in using the procedures of spiritualism without believing in the least in the principle of spiritualism, employing the language of occultism without adhering to its inspiration, venerating superstitions without sympathizing with the clumsy homage man's consciousness renders across their apparent puerility to the unknown, accomplishing the step of metaphysics while bringing its evidence down to that of simple beauty. These procedures, this language, this step, always erroneous in the form they borrow and—if we may say so—in their objectivication, nevertheless express an exigency that surrealism wakens, but risks deceiving. Those who abandon the marvelous expectation for despair or to submit themselves blindly to the forces of history, have they not been victims of that philosophy of immanence that surrealism, with its humanist scruple, has never wanted to deny?

I think for my part that in the metaphysical affirmation

of transcendence man finds his most authentic verity. And I am sure that away from all superstition and dogmatism, that affirmation can be founded integrally in reason; the eternal philosophical critique, demonstrating that no known object has meaning or reality except relative to our knowledge, suffices to establish the transcendence of Being as supreme certitude. But the surrealist evidence is not metaphysical; it wishes to remain human, and thus poetic. Still, of all poets, the surrealists appear the closest to metaphysics. More exactly, they reveal that, metaphysics apart, poetry is for man the road leading closest to the truth, provided its language remains scrupulously faithful to the truth of man. The work of André Breton is without doubt the most perfect and admirable example of this scrupulous fidelity in our century. This is why Breton seems in spite of himself a messenger of transcendence. He is inspired by Engels, but he recovers Plato. He declares that he would like it if his life "left behind it no other murmur but the song of a watcher, a song to beguile expectation." [108] But far from beguiling expectation, Breton's words direct it toward its essential goal. Confusion of the object with Being, of philosophy with system, forgetfulness of death and forgetfulness of love, reduction of knowledge to positive science and of man's powers to technological action, purely aesthetic concern for form and exercises in style, falsely justified abandon to the crimes of history—all these modern forms of the spirit's resignation are shaken at his appeal. Surrealism derealizes the objective world, if not by affirmation of Being, at least in the name of an expected happiness. Encounters and signs indicate that there are other ways of comprehending the World than those of a sterilizing intellectualism and announce an advent whose foreboding has at least the merit of rousing those who thought they could measure the real in terms of scientific experience. In the uneasiness a coincidence inspires in us, in the light of an analogy that reveals, for example, the relation of a face and a landscape, we understand that quantitative interpretation of the real cannot take the place of "qualitative" interpretation.[109] Breton expects from the revolution that the "artificial precariousness of the social condition" will no longer disguise "the real precariousness" of the "human condition." We may say that, since surrealism, nothing any longer obscures this need "which cannot be situated in time," [110] by which man is defined.

And yet we must recognize that, tearing us from the diversion of objective knowledge and history, surrealism is not willing to render us the unease properly metaphysical. The surreal does not appear in it as a sign of Being; it results always, inside human frontiers, from putting desire in relation to representation. And certainly the conflict of desire and representation is the essential drama of man having come to objective knowledge. At the instinctual stage, desire is structure and informs its environment. The primitive consciousness still maintains its direct contact with Nature when it wants to act by charms. But the preeminence of visual representation, which presupposes distancing the object, the coming of an analytical intelligence that destroys every form and recomposes the real according to its own laws, binds desire in its solitude and engages us in a history in which from then on all things bear the mark of separation. Here the end is distinguished from the means, any action assumes waiting and subordination of the pleasure to the reality principle; the tendency, abandoned by the form it inhabited, must be subjected to abstract rules, and man perceives around him that image of the World which he must then reckon with. To end this split, surrealism tries to reconcile desire and representation. But despite its hope in the future, it is mainly by a return to the inner that it conceives this reconciliation. Not that properly speaking it wishes to return to a problematic native self-consciousness. But agreeing to define man as the being who imagines, seeing in imagination the most evident sign of our freedom, surrealism hopes to subject again to the powers of desire a group of images that are only formed, however, by the very rupture with desire.

Thanks to the eruption of mad images—and it hardly knows, moreover, whether they manifest the form of our needs or the caprice of their own spontaneity—it attempts to break the coherence of the stable images that constitute the objective World, the World of science and of positive reason. It seeks objects coming mysteriously to fulfill our hopes,[111] and when it does not find them, it constructs a sort of counter-object which, far from supporting physical laws, materializes our unconscious desires or connives with a symbolic function putting our sexual tendencies into play.[112] It gives itself over to automatism, accepts madness because there desire is already master of representation, and is tempted by sadism, in which pure subjective exigency is irritated to such a point by the exteriority and independence of the loved image that it does not hesitate to break it, to destroy it. And such, in effect, is the last word of man reduced to himself. We can, however, draw other lessons from our sorrows, our solitude. Renouncing the "green paradise of childish loves," [113] many philosophers have meditated on the essence of separation that every image, every objective representation, contains. If our glance sees only at a distance, if all knowledge opposes the subject with an object, if all thought is exerted in a time which we know already contains the hour of our death, must we not recognize that our condition signifies, indeed makes perfectly obvious, that essential absence, that transcendence of Being of which all true metaphysics has never been anything but the reminder? Science forgets the absence of Being. Poetry consoles us for it by producing, in the imaginary, the illusion of immanence that we call beauty. Metaphysics is discourse about the absence. In it, spirit separates itself from man, refuses to regard man as a principle, rises to the incomprehensible beyond that man does not contain but only signifies. Surrealism can lead to such a philosophy. But such is not the philosophy of surrealism.

Postscript and Notes on Joë Bousquet

Conflicts and Abandonments

Considering only the philosophy of surrealism in the preceding pages, I have given no place to anecdotes. Thus, I have not spoken of the conflicts, the ruptures, the abandonments that many a time disrupted what is called the surrealist "group." But incidents in the history of surrealism are so often brought forward with intentions of denigration that I cannot pass over them in silence and give the reader the impression that generally I approve what is said.

There is certainly no question of forgetting how important personal considerations have sometimes been in the history of surrealism, much less of supposing those quarrels fortunate that made only the enemies of surrealism rejoice. But we must realize that the conflicts between surrealists were the inevitable consequence of extreme seriousness, of a scrupulous will to purity. All of man and all of man's consciousness are concerned in surrealism. The values at stake are moral, not literary. Is it so surprising, then, that there was some intolerance in their affirmation?

Further, most of the surrealist "affairs" expressed a conflict within surrealism itself, a conflict which—brought down to its essence—shows the laceration of man reduced to himself. Can there be a coherent atheism? Can there be an optimism without transcendence? Such are the problems a conceptual analysis of each conflict invariably comes up with. Existence and poetry, reality principle and pleasure principle, revolutionary will and contemplative ecstasy of love seem, indeed, to be contradictory, and surrealism maintains them together only by heroic tension that sometimes gives way to oscillation or choice. And certainly to abandon the tension that maintains the contradictory surrealist values is to abandon surrealism itself. In this connection Breton is correct in writing that in 1930 Aragon, about 1935 Dali, and in 1938 Eluard "ceased to be surrealists." [1] But we must add that those who objectively renounced surrealism have not always denounced the values they most highly regarded in surrealism as they understood it.

So it is not without reason that Léon-Gabriel Gros esteems "that in the light of what he has written later, we can measure how much Eluard's thought has evolved logically." [2] Eluard never entirely accepted the essential affirmations of surrealism; from 1926 we can see in him signs of a coming rupture. On the other hand, after that rupture, Eluard did not condemn his past activity. I saw Eluard often during the occupation and at the liberation, when divisions in the Resistance were already revealing that the combat that had united us against a state of things we thought unacceptable was, nevertheless, not the same combat, had not been undertaken in view of the same goals. I remember our conversations at my place or in his apartment in the Rue de la Chapelle or sometimes in the home of my friend the painter André Beaudin, with whom he had done *Doubles d'ombre*,[3] a work in which the most moving poems and the most sensitive drawings illuminate each other by an identical rigorousness. Eluard always insisted, in the most formal way, that he had renounced nothing he once loved. I am not writing this to add gossip to gossip, but as witness and proof. In 1945 Eluard asked me write an article affirming the continuity of surrealism and of the Resistance. I gave him the article and he published it in *Action*.[4] The evolution of the surrealists become poets of the Resistance, I said, "far from involving a change of attitude, expresses a single design." And here are the conclusions of that short study: "We can say of all surrealism that it tended to give us a more complete and more exact image of man, from the surrealism of the collages, of the chance dialogues and automatic writing. An idea of human powers was proposed here, which far surpassed mere powers of artistic creation. The imaginary tended, with all its weight, to become real, and man's dreams to transform the world.

"One of the most interesting things about surrealism is in fact how it attempted always to present a total and complete man, affirming by that a confident humanism without fetters and without limits, where the excitement of the marvelous and the legends of childhood retain their significance and their value and avoid all foreign exploitation. Going over the pages of Breton, the poems of Eluard, the texts of Aragon, the books of images by Max Ernst, contemplating the pictures of Tanguy and Magritte, we shall see that these works tend not only to resolve by new means literary or pictorial problems, but to enlarge the human domain, to liberate unknown and unconscious forces that are in man, to render to man and man alone all that belongs to him, that is to say all that he can think and dream and conceive.

"To liberate man was always the aim of surrealism. Is it necessary to add that with Nazism menacing, in the midst of an oppressed France, the problem of man's liberation could not be resolved by automatic writing, but in a manner more precise, urgent, and pointed, by taking a political position and by a call to arms. The change came because of circumstances, but the goal remained the same. From *Capitale de la douleur* to *Rendezvous allemand* Eluard has written many poems. These poems always illustrate the same idea, inscribe on all the pages the same name, express a single thought."

Even if one does not approve what I wrote then (and still think),[5] he will certainly agree that Eluard's publication of my article indicated a clear wish in him not to renounce surrealism. This is why, two years later, I could state in a lecture read at the Collège Philosophique and printed in their bulletin: "It seems characteristic to me to see the surrealists now divided and having chosen, like the romantics of yesteryear, some a social action without dreams, others an attitude less renouncing their first ideal, but also with less engagement. And I believe nonetheless that all were faithful. But hard reality will show that one cannot be faithful to everything he has sworn to keep when between the objects chosen there are contradictions that the mere desire for total synthesis is not sufficient to resolve.... The dimension of ethics and the dimension of history cannot be reconciled." [6] Now André Breton, in his *Entretiens,* without being of the same opinion, declares himself "greatly impressed" by this and says it "bears the stamp of wisdom." [7] Of all Breton's appreciations of my writings, this one most pleased me. I am certainly not forgetting that it was for not repudiating my letter to him (March 7, 1933) that Breton was dismissed from the Association of Revolutionary Writers and Artists.[8] But I happen to be moved, even more than by interhuman loyalty, by such fidelity to impersonal truth, truth that we should in fact prefer to our friends and to ourselves. "Beyond all that has separated us," Breton writes, thinking of those who have left him, beyond "the passions that have entered here— some of which are far from spent—my desire would be to reach that point of serenity from which one contemplates the road taken together, from where one is thankful without reservations for what has united in the greatest fervor a certain number of men around a common cause, even when those men have not always been the same ones...." [9] Think of the strictness always displayed by the man who wrote those lines. Here that strictness itself, without being repudiated, seems to be passed toward what prompted it. It is by such movements that Breton is, in the most rigorous sense of the word, a philosopher. And among the philosophers of today, how rare are those who remember that their first duty is to prefer truth even to their love of truth!

The Unity of Joë Bousquet

Since I am here in a personal account and on the border-lines of emotion and of confidences, I cannot end this book without mentioning the room in Carcassonne where Joë Bousquet, bedridden since 1917 as a result of his wound, received his friends, most of whom were also mine. I recall seeing there Claude Estève, Pierre Sire, Franz Molino, René Nelli, Maria Sire, Henri Féraud, Jean Ballard who often came from Marseille, Max Ernst who sometimes came from Paris, Carlo Suarès, and many besides. It was there I first discovered surrealism. The walls of the room were covered with paintings by Tanguy, Ernst, Masson, Dali, Miro, and the appearance of each number of the *Révolution surréaliste* came to fulfill an expectation and seemed to bear a message. Can Bousquet be called a surrealist? He realized, in any case, that sort of unity of man that in many respects surrealism sought; in him dream and perception were truly identical. Moreover, from that identity there resulted a great obscurity in his writings; the language, ceaselessly turning back upon itself, left the reader before pure opacity. This is what I noted, for example, with regard to *Rendez-vous d'un soir d'hiver*.[10] "The author," I wrote, "wants to attain by love to a mystical knowledge of the world. But his book differs from the mystical works to which we are accustomed in that, first of all, it disconcerts and seems to mask a failure. Could that come from the fact that the loved woman, being here the end of all seeking and yet remaining woman and yet loved, hinders the lover with all her exteriority from attaining the unity toward which he tends? Nothing of the kind. Annie's reality is that of the world and there is no dualism. But while the mystics conduct us in general only to the borders of their experience and claim that it is unspeakable, Bousquet attempts to communicate his. Now this enterprise is, strictly, unrealizable, since language, by essence discursive, cannot express the unity of an intuition. So in Bousquet's book there are contradictions, phrases that fall away, and as if set toward obscurity. Language in fact must there negate itself at each step, so that what it has separated can be united. But let one abandon oneself to these contradictions that deliver us from the various, and he will perceive that the world of love is at hand: it is the real world, the world of matter—from which we are absent— where things have taken the place of their names."

I again affirmed this unity of Bousquet in a note I wrote in 1947 for the *Journal des poètes*,[11] in which Bousquet told me he recognized himself completely. I evoke there our first interview:

"I was eighteen when I first met Joë Bousquet. The day before I was still afraid of the encounter that I was told was necessary. Uneasy adolescent, dissatisfied with myself, I was protesting a fate that seemed to me encountered from without. But I detested in others this way of not being oneself, which nevertheless made up my life. And what could that man be whom the course of the world had so strictly cut off from itself? I imagined him still occupied with his foiled plans, perhaps rebelling, perhaps escaping himself, perhaps finally resigned and asking from willpower the self-harmony that an accident had broken. Any solution for him seemed to me non-coincidental or of a constructed coincidence.

"I have known Bousquet for more than twenty years. And it is always of him I think when I want to persuade myself that nothing is unjust and that the unity of man is possible. Bousquet is undivided being. It must not be concealed that, by that fact itself, he irritates. But not by his faults—it is in perceiving that the friendship one bears him is itself impure. Because in dominating we always love, what we cherish in our friends is their vulnerability. Their faults, I mean to the extent they are open to us, permit us that community of weakness that is called conscious communication. Here we are consoling, compassionate, desirous of healing, avid to render the other still more miserable.

"Bousquet discourages these impure games. This does not make him easy to like. He has no destiny, for he is his destiny. He has not been injured, for he is his injury. I do not call him stoic, wanting what he is, but one, being what he is. Nothing is more laughable than the opinion that he is 'a modern author.' For no one is less than he of this idiotic age, where men are constructed by concepts, take for their real drama that of their thoughts and go from reflection to life. The essential obscurity of Bousquet's texts is not the fabricated obscurity nowadays fashionable. And nothing is more vain than wanting to explicate these texts by going behind what is obvious in them to find the concepts from which they were born. For they are not offspring of consciousness, but of nature. Bousquet has no system. The system is born from seeking in objects a unity that the self does not discover in itself. Bousquet is one; his wound has made him invulnerable, incomprehensible. It has conferred on him the beauty of those forces which we record without having to think, for they are of the order of being and not of the order of spirit.

"Bousquet does not construct himself, does not express himself; he is manifested. Before knowing him I feared that the separation within oneself that in man we call consciousness would have in him the aspect of a wound, rather than an opening onto the world. In fact Bousquet is not open to the world, but it is because he is not separated from himself. His body takes the place of consciousness. His richness is in it; he is himself a world, he is absolute creator. He has taught me everything and has taught me nothing. I owe him no idea; I owe him knowing what without him I would never have known: his admirable words, closed, perfect, reveal to me that he is the being for which all consciousness longs. No doubt he will never know completely what he was for me and for all those who had the unique chance to see and hear him."

Bousquet, even so, had to evolve. Toward the end of his life, Jean Paulhan became almost his sole master. Paulhan persuaded him that he should substitute in his preoccupations the problem of language for that of being. But the character of Bousquet was such that, from this new point of view, he found again, in another style, his unity. He intended to coincide, this time, with the events of his life, considered as a sort of language and, if I may put it so, as the absolute of the problem. And his past work itself would be illuminated with a new light. I tried, after Joë Bousquet's death, to understand him as, in his last days, he wanted to be understood. I reproduce here, to end this book, the last lines that I wrote on my friend. One will find in them, I think, the theme of the identity of man and his fate that we have so often encountered in surrealism. But the negation of transcendence seems to me more striking yet in Joë Bousquet than in Breton. Bousquet tries to reduce himself entirely to events.[12] Breton considers "that what I take for objective manifestations of my existence . . . are only what happens in the limits of this life of an activity whose true field is totally unknown to me. . . ." [13] He seems then to appeal to the transcendence that elsewhere he denies. And I believe that this implicit appeal to transcendence is what distinguishes Breton most profoundly from those who left surrealism, whether, like Aragon or Eluard, for political action or, like Leiris, Queneau, and Bousquet, for the concern with pure language. Whether he evokes against the latter the unknown that our life merely expresses or, meeting the former, judges history according to the vertical dimension of ethics and refuses to justify the means by the end, Breton always recovers the truth of metaphysics. And this is why, engaged in paths that are not his, I have been able in this book to recognize in André Breton one of my thinking-masters.

Joë Bousquet and the Ethic of Language [14]

No idea has cast more of a shadow over the creations of the spirit than that of vocation. It masks the relation between men and their lives; it leads to the supposition that the poet or the philosopher has a sort of message anterior to his existence, expressing itself without regard to daily difficulties and as if in spite of them. To speak of vocation is always to take the side of revolt, to prefer a man to his life, to believe there was more richness in his dream than in his history. It is always closing one's eyes.

Joë Bousquet's eyes were open. "The only morality I retain," he writes, "is that which ... imposes on us, as sole principle of entire existence, the fact that comes to us, whatever it is, holds that event alone is real, it being our part to accomplish its perfection and splendor." [15] Those who knew Bousquet know how scrupulously he followed this rule, his only rule. If his life was beautiful and to this extent seductive, it was because, far from wanting to make it his work, he found his basis in it.

Without the accident of his wound, Bousquet would doubtless never have written. We cannot therefore speak of an innate mission, a first intuition of the World and of man. But, wounded, Bousquet considered his wound as a sort of birth, annulling his birth in the flesh. "I escaped," he says, "from the mortal consequences of a shock, to render doubtful the dispositions my birth had given me. By untiring labor I substituted for me a cultured being." [16] So, mortally wounded, he seemed to us no longer mortal. He had ceased to be a child of Nature to become one of events. Of all future events, he seemed to us then to have to remain the consciousness and the echo.

And such was the sense of his work. With anyone else literary concerns would have been evasion, compensation. One can forget a misfortune in the exercise of an art with borrowed forms and in the pleasures of vanity the exercise provides. Bousquet's genius was, on the contrary, to understand that by the effects of his wound separation had become his essence. His wound had made him a poet; he was to consecrate his poetry, not to forgetting it but to deepening it. "I put all my strength into naturalizing the accident that victimized my youth. I wanted it to cease to be outside me." [17]

Bousquet followed out the rigor of such a project, which led him to an ethic of language. In expressing it he placed the value with the expressed, leaving the inwardness to dissolve in the visible and the experienced sadness in the light of the object. "I know," he says, "that death and unhappiness are images." [18] The poems of Bousquet, René Nelli writes, "express all the reduction of oneself to the event." [19] Here is the key to these obscure texts that always seem to close upon themselves. To learn to read them, we must understand to what point the reduction Nelli speaks of was imposed by the necessity of a fate that Bousquet wanted to accept, to the extent of becoming it.

Each man must choose between the search for a paradise lost, which seems to him like his being, and the difficult effort by which he identifies with the object, with history, that is to say, with the truth of a discourse. Bousquet thus opposes knowledge and existence: "The apotheosis of knowledge excludes existence." [20] And if he complains of writing with difficulty, it is not in order to deplore some crudeness, but to signify that the act of writing engages his life, separating it from its being. "What dominates this close of the year," we read in his diary, "is the crushing conviction that I understand nothing of my art. I do not know how to write." [21] This apparently banal uneasiness soon reveals its depths: "I am not the author of what I have done passably well. One could say that the effort expended in expressing myself aggravates the misunderstanding between my thought and me."

And Bousquet certainly expresses here a difficulty common to all writers. But instead of deploring the insufficiency of words and taking refuge by a facile movement in some ineffable experience, he prefers language to himself and, with language, the objective tissue of his life: "It displeases me to feel more real than the thought to which I long to submit." [22] He knows that thought, being discourse, is closer to event than to being; events may be spoken, their nature is that of words. Here Bousquet accepts, consents, "I sought for all the facts that made me fall under the domination of my words." [23]

This ethic of language explains, I think, how at the end of his life Bousquet occupied himself almost exclusively with the work of Jean Paulhan. I believe also that his reserves with regard to Cartesian thought had their deeper source there. He did not fall into the error of those who see in that thought only the transparency of clear ideas; rather, he was disquieted to see Descartes accord being to thought. Of the "I think, therefore I am" he once wrote me, "What will you answer if I tell you that off and on I sense, to the point of madness, that I am being thought?" "I feel the idea of self nourish itself on the things that happen to me. . . ." And elsewhere: "I do not think of describing objects. I put myself in front of them, until I am not regarding them, but they see me and invent in my eyes their own image which would put me to sleep at their feet."

So in this age in which existentialists and linguistic philosophers violently disagree, Bousquet was able to find in the objective event and in the language that describes it the reason for his very existence. His asceticism was not that of a hermit who had voluntarily forsaken the world, but of a lover whom the world had for-

172 The Philosophy of Surrealism

saken and who could find the world again only by
preferring it to himself, searching only in the splendor of
things for the essence of his sorrows. Nothing is farther
from this authentic quest of being by the word than the
artificial creation of works from concepts so common in
our day. This is where Bousquet was like no one else.
He was not of those who go from reflection to life and
take for their drama that of their thoughts. He had rather
find, with the aid of images and words, his lost life and
avoid sterile revolt by preferring what he saw and what
he said to what he was. So he was always consoling, not
by the illusion of some promise, but by the truth of
reconciliation. In the cemetery of Villalier, where we
accompanied him on a morning of rain and sunshine,
he seemed to welcome us, to have taken the form and
the colors of a landscape he had loved more than he
loved himself. And I would be faithful to him in no
longer seeking the truth of his voice but in those I still
hear, or the exactitude of his thoughts but in the World's
visage.

Notes

[*All books mentioned in the Notes were published in Paris unless otherwise noted.*]

Introduction

1. [Maurice Nadeau, *Histoire du surréalisme* and *Documents surréalistes*, Ed. du Seuil, 1945 and 1948.]
2. [*Rencontre* and *hasard objectif* are, as it were, technical terms in surrealism. See Chapter Three and Breton's *Nadja*.]

Chapter One

1. André Breton, *Poisson soluble*, text 1, pp. 79–80, following *Manifeste du surréalisme*, Ed. du Sagittaire, Simon Kra, 1924.
2. André Breton, *Lettre à combat*, 19 May 1949, reprinted in *Flagrant délit* (Thésée, 1949) and again in *La Clé des champs*, Sagittaire, 1953, p. 173.
3. "Holed up as far as possible in this impeccable black coat that I have not taken off since" (*Poisson soluble*, text 1, p. 81) and "it had been admitted carelessly that the beautiful white palpitating breasts had never belonged to a living creature of the species that still haunts our desires." (*Ibid.*, text 3, p. 88.)
4. "The value of the image depends on the beauty of the spark obtained." (*Manifeste du surréalisme*, p. 59.)
5. *Flagrant délit*, in *La Clé des champs*, p. 136.
6. André Breton, *Entretiens*, N.R.F., 1952, p. 77. On this activity, see Chapter Two.
7. *Manifeste*, pp. 47–48.

8. "Childhood perhaps comes closest to the 'real life.'" *Ibid.*, p. 63. Breton is using Rimbaud's phrase: "Real life is absent." (*Une Saison en enfer*, Délires, I.)

9. *Ibid.*, p. 74.

10. *Poisson soluble*, text 1, p. 79.

11. *Ibid.*, text 22, p. 141.

12. *Ibid.*, text 7, p. 100.

13. On the lover's madness, see e.g., Plato *Phaedrus* 249D ff.

14. ". . . a new body, a body like one assuredly never seen before, never caressed before . . ." "the boat in pursuit of the new Eve had never returned. . . ." "She was beyond our desires. . . ." (*Poisson soluble*, text 26, p. 158.)

15. *Ibid.*, text 7, p. 98.

16. "I have no heart for the earth." *Ibid.*, text 26, p. 158.

17. *Ibid.*, text 23, pp. 145–46.

18. I have grave reservations about the supposed "surrealist pessimism." (Breton, Reply to Jean Duché, *Figaro Littéraire*, 5 Oct. 1946; reprinted in *Entretiens*, p. 248.)

19. *Poisson soluble*, text 7, pp. 97–98.

20. Questionnaire in *La Revolution surréaliste*, no. 12, 15 Dec. 1929.

21. *La Revolution surréaliste*, no. 8, 1 Dec. 1926, text by Pierre Unik, p. 3. Cf. in no. 7 the text of Antonin Artaud: The anvil of forces: "The odor of nothingness, smell of the absurd, dunghill of death entire . . . I too await only the wind. Whether it is called love or misery, it will hardly ground me except on a shore of bones."

22. *Ibid.*, text of Cl.-A. Puget, pp. 3–4.

23. *Manifeste*, p. 27.

24. See *ibid.*, p. 42. They were Aragon, Baron, Boiffard, Breton, Carrive, Crevel, Delteil, Desnos, Eluard, Gérard, Limbour, Malkine, Morise, Naville, Noll, Péret, Picon, Soupault, Vitrac.

25. Paul Eluard, Prière d'insérer for *Les Dessous d'une vie ou La Pyramide humaine*, 1926. Cf. *Donner à voir*, Gallimard, 1939, p. 147.

26. Georges Hugnet, Introduction to *Petite anthologie poétique du surréalisme*, Jeanne Bucher, 1934, p. 21. Besides, Hugnet perceives perfectly well that the aim of

surrealism is opposed to this distinction and notes that there is a point where the poem "coincides with the dream and with automatism" and "is fused with them."

27. Eluard, *Capitale de la douleur,* Gallimard, 1926, "L'égalité des sexes," p. 49.
28. *Ibid.,* "Denise disait aux merveilles," p. 65.
29. *Ibid.,* "Ta bouche aux lèvres d'or," p. 140.
30. *Ibid.,* "La courbe de tes yeux," p. 143.
31. Racine, *Phèdre,* act V, scene 7.
32. Breton, *Manifeste,* p. 45.
33. *Ibid.,* p. 71.
34. Aragon, *Traité du style,* Gallimard, 1928, p. 188.
35. *Ibid.,* p. 85.
36. *Ibid.,* p. 105.
37. Breton, *Les Pas perdus,* N.R.F., 1924, p. 8.
38. Breton, *Manifeste,* p. 9.
39. *Ibid.,* p. 12.
40. *Poisson soluble,* text 1, p. 77. A poem in *Clair de terre* (1923) was already called "Not Every Paradise Is Lost."
41. *Manifeste,* p. 30.
42. See *Entretiens,* p. 220. This sentence, read by Gide to Breton, seemed to him "somewhat debatable."
43. Bossuet, *Méditations sur l'Evangile,* Sermon on the Mount, first day.
44. Breton, *Le Revolver à cheveux blancs,* Le Cahiers Libres, 1932, "There is no exit from here," p. 56. The poem had already appeared in *Clair de terre.*
45. *Poisson soluble,* text 11, p. 109.
46. *Ibid.,* text 26, p. 153.
47. *Ibid.,* text 26, p. 157.
48. *Ibid.,* text 28, p. 163.
49. *Ibid.,* text 18, p. 129.
50. *Ibid.,* text 32, p. 180.
51. Breton, *Les Pas perdus,* p. 7.
52. "There are some lousy pricks who speak with papal solemnity about departing. . . ." (Aragon, *Traité du style,* p. 81); "the buggers who roll their eyes when they pronounce the word adventure" (*ibid.,* p. 82);

". . . escape. Sweet perspective, less and less dramatic, as it is generalized and becomes more idiotic" (*ibid.,* p. 82).

53. "The Mysterious Corset" in *Le Revolver à cheveux blancs,* p. 31. (The poem is much earlier and had appeared, in 1919, in *Mont-de-Piété,* Au Sans Pareil.)

54. Breton, *Nadja,* Gallimard, 1928, p. 31.

55. *Ibid.,* p. 165.

56. Thus, on the Place Dauphine: "It is, no mistake, the sex of Paris that is sketched under its shadows. Its fleece burns yet, sometime during the year, from the torture of the Templars that took place there March 13, 1313, which some people say had much to do in the revolutionary fate of the town." (Le Pont-Neuf, in *La Clé des champs,* p. 232.)

57. *Ibid.,* p. 230.

58. *Les Pas perdus,* p. 12.

59. Breton, *Entretiens,* p. 10.

60. "There are some port wines the taste of which is not bad, but somehow unstable. The palate does not retain them. They flee, leaving no memory. This is not the case with port from Certa: warm, firm, assured and truly sonorous." (Aragon, *Le Paysan de Paris,* Gallimard, 1926, p. 95.) Cf.: "This soup, true panade of concentrated onion, was served piping hot . . . under a layer, thick and solid, of Gruyère and parmesan. It was au gratin, golden yellow. . . ." (Léon Daudet, *Paris vécu,* premiere serie, Gallimard, 1929.)

61. *Le Paysan de Paris,* p. 49. "A whole year I bit hair of fern . . ." etc.

62. "You have encountered . . . these mad women, the first from the Nord-Sud, about five o'clock. How many times have you felt a marriage on the traveling woman's finger? But she was looking for nothing but a passing breach. The human sky has its lightning bolts, untraceable." (*Ibid.,* pp. 64–65.)

63. "O my golden image, here I am; let everything finally fall apart in the palace of illusions and of silence. The woman docilely espouses my wishes and anticipates them . . ." (*Ibid.,* p. 130.)

64. *Nadja,* p. 38.

65. Aragon, *Traité du style,* pp. 188–89.

66. Hugnet, Introduction to the *Petite anthologie poétique du surréalisme*, pp. 18–19.
67. Jean Paulhan, *Les Fleurs de Tarbes*, Gallimard, 1941, pp. 38–39.
68. Breton, *L'Amour fou*, Gallimard, 1937, pp. 149–66.
69. [Translated as *La Renarde*, after the pet fox in the novel.]
70. *Manifeste*, pp. 31–32 (and *Entrée des médiums*, see below).
71. *Ibid.*, pp. 35–36.
72. Aragon, "Une Vague de rêves," *Commerce*, no. 2 (1924–25).
73. Breton, *Entrée des médiums*. Article in *Littérature*, reprinted in *Les Pas perdus*, pp. 147–58.
74. *Les Pas perdus*, pp. 152–53.
75. *Ibid.*, p. 156.
76. *Ibid.*, p. 158.
77. Breton, *Entretiens*, p. 84.
78. *Ibid.*, p. 90.
79. Maurice Nadeau, *Histoire du surréalisme*, p. 91.
80. Claude Bernard, *Introduction à l'étude de la médecine expérimentale*, Part I, chapter 1, sec. 5.
81. Breton, *Entretiens*, p. 75.
82. Breton, Le Message automatique, in *Point du jour*, Gallimard, 1934, pp. 217–51.
83. Breton reproduced several of these drawings in *Minotaure*, 3–4.
84. Breton, *Entreteins*, p. 79.
85. Breton, *Point du jour*, p. 219.
86. *Ibid.*, p. 220.
87. *Entretiens*, p. 83.
88. ". . . whoever has not seen his pencil settle on the paper, without the least hesitation and with prodigious rapidity, these stunning poetic equations . . . can have no idea of all that that involved then, of the absolute oracular value that that held." (Breton, *Nadja*, pp. 36–37.)
89. Baudelaire, "L'Invitation au voyage," in *Les Fleurs du Mal*.
90. *Point du jour*, p. 237.

91. *Traité du style*, p. 208: "Only meaning of the word Beyond, you are in poetry. . . ."

92. Breton, *Devant le rideau*, Introduction to *Le Surréalisme en 1947* (presentation of the International Exposition of Surrealism, Maeght), text reprinted in *La Clé des champs*, p. 94.

93. *Ibid.*, p. 95.

94. See *Les Pas perdus*, p. 158.

95. *Point du jour*, p. 246.

96. *Entretiens*, p. 82.

97. *Point du jour*, p. 217.

98. *Ibid.*, p. 241.

99. *Ibid.*, p. 244.

100. *Entretiens*, p. 82.

101. Quoting and approving Professor Lipps, Breton declares: "Hypnosis is never anything but the negative reason of the talents manifested under its influence; their real source is to be found in the tendencies, faculties, or dispositions which were already existing but fettered . . . hypnosis is limited to liberating them." And automatic writing seems to realize "an assured means of encouraging the treasure of psychic faculties, especially of artistic talent." (*Point du jour*, pp. 242–43.)

102. *Entretiens*, p. 10.

103. *Ibid.*, p. 11.

104. *Ibid.*, p. 12.

105. Poem published in the *Phalange*, 1914, reprinted in *Mont-de-Piété*.

106. *L'Amour fou*, p. 170.

107. *Traité du style*, pp. 60–61.

108. *Manifeste*, p. 24.

109. *Ibid.*, p. 18.

110. *Ibid.*, p. 12 ff.

111. *Ibid.*, p. 14.

112. *L'Amour fou*, p. 14. Cf. in *Mont-de-Piété*, the poem "Black Forest."

113. *L'Amour fou*, p. 12.

114. *Ibid.*, p. 13.

115. Descartes' *Discours de la méthode* also proposes to universalize a science assuring man a mastery (in the case of Descartes, the technological mastery of Nature).

116. *Manifeste,* p. 42.
117. Jules Monnerot, *La Poésie moderne et le sacré,* Gallimard, 1945, pp. 41–42.
118. "I believe in the future resolution of these two states of dream and reality, seemingly so contradictory, in a sort of absolute reality, of surreality." Breton, *Manifeste,* pp. 23–24.
119. Monnerot, *La Poésie moderne et le sacré,* pp. 17–18.
120. See *ibid.,* p. 16.
121. *Point du jour,* p. 124.
122. Poem taken from *Mont-de-Piété* (1913), cited in *Entretiens,* p. 8.
123. Tristan Tzara, *Essai sur la situation de la poésie,* in *Le surréalisme au service de la Révolution,* no. 4, Dec. 1931.
124. See *Littérature,* Mar. 1921, and *Entretiens,* p. 66.
125. Paul Bénichou, *Morales du grand siècle,* Gallimard, 1948.
126. *Manifeste,* pp. 43–44.
127. *Ibid.,* p. 42.
128. *Point du jour,* p. 240.
129. Michel Carrouges, *André Breton et les données fondamentales du surréalisme,* Gallimard. 1950, p. 10.
130. Breton, *Plûtot la vie,* poem from *Clair de terre,* reprinted in *Le Revolver à cheveux blancs,* p. 67.
131. Breton, *Position politique du surréalisme,* Sagittaire, 1935, p. 36.
132. *Manifeste,* p. 10.
133. Reply to "Ouvrez-vous?" in *Médium,* new series, no. 1, Nov. 1953, p. 12.
134. *Les Pas perdus,* p. 10.
135. Breton, *Second manifeste du surréalisme,* Kra, 1930, p. 24.
136. *Ibid.,* p. 19.
137. Hegel's method, Breton says, "has beaten all others into indigence. Where the Hegelian dialectic does not work, there is for me no thought, no hope of truth." (*Entretiens,* p. 152.)
138. Jean Hyppolite, *Logique et existence,* P.U.F., 1953, pp. 70–71. The phrases in italics are from Hegel.
139. Poem reprinted in *Le Revolver à cheveux blancs,* p. 65.

140. "Rendez-vous," poem from *Clair de terre*, reprinted in *Le Revolver à cheveux blancs*, p. 54.

141. Baudelaire, "L'Invitation au voyage," in *Les Fleurs du mal*.

142. *Manifeste*, p. 63. Cf. "That lost fatherland of mental freedom where we could, as children, wander, play. ..." (André and Marcel Jean, "Mourir pour la patrie," *Le Surréalisme au service de la Révolution* no. 6, p. 47.)

143. *Manifeste*, p. 7.

144. *Ibid.*, p. 8.

145. *Médium*, new series, no. 1, Nov. 1953, p. 16.

Chapter Two

1. Albert Camus, *L'Homme révolté*, Gallimard, 1951, pp. 118–19.

2. *Ibid.*, p. 120.

3. *Ibid.*, p. 122.

4. Ernest Gengenbach, *Surréalisme et christianisme*, published by the author, 1938, p. 14.

5. Claude Mauriac, *André Breton*, Editions de Flore, 1949, p. 160.

6. *Ibid.*, p. 162.

7. *A la niche les glapisseurs de Dieu*, Editions surréalistes, 1948, p. 13.

8. Claude Mauriac, *André Breton*, p. 162.

9. Michel Carrouges, *La Mystique du surhomme*, Gallimard, 1948, p. 34.

10. Nietzsche, *Also Sprach Zarathustra* [in the Hanser edition, II, 340].

11. Carrouges, *La Mystique du surhomme*, p. 34.

12. Carrouges, *André Breton et les données fondamentales du surréalisme*, p. 39.

13. I call humanism what Gabriel Rey calls superhumanism. To say that "all things are immanent to man, that he can integrate everything, Nature and Spirit, natural and supernatural, real and surreal" is, in effect, for Rey, to be a superhumanist. (See Gabriel Rey, *Humanisme et surhumanisme*, Hachette, 1951, p. 255.) This is merely a difference of vocabulary. However, Rey perhaps insists too little on the critical lucidity of surrealism, which the present work tries to bring out.

14. *L'Amour fou,* p. 108.

15. *Point du jour,* p. 84.

16. *Arcane 17,* Brentano's, New York, 1945, p. 11.

17. *Ibid.,* p. 175.

18. Julien Gracq, *André Breton,* José Corti, 1948, pp. 39–41.

19. Victor Crastre, *André Breton,* Arcanes, 1952, p. 43.

20. *Manifeste,* p. 44. On the always considerable influence of Vaché on surrealism, cf. for example in *Médium,* no. 3, May 1954, the article by Jean Schuster, "Tout de même, tout de même!"

21. Gracq, *André Breton,* p. 31. J.-L. Bédouin goes so far as to think that "Vaché is not essentially distinct from Breton." (Jean-Louis Bédouin, *André Breton,* Seghers, 1950, p. 51.) I am persuaded otherwise.

22. [Appollinaire's "surrealist drama" (1918).]

23. *Second manifeste,* p. 12.

24. *Les Pas perdus,* pp. 67–72.

25. *Ibid.,* p. 9.

26. *Ibid.,* p. 8.

27. *Ibid.,* p. 24.

28. *La Révolution surréaliste,* no. 1, Dec. 1924.

29. The text of this declaration will be found in Nadeau, *Histoire du surréalisme,* pp. 104–5 and *Documents surréalistes,* pp. 42–43.

30. *La Révolution surréaliste,* no. 3, Apr. 1925.

31. Breton, "Pourquoi je prends la direction de la Révolution surréaliste," *La Révolution surréaliste,* no. 4, July 1925.

32. Aragon, fragments of a lecture, reproduced in *La Révolution surréaliste,* no. 4.

33. Dialogue between Breton and Aimé Patri in *Arts,* 16 Nov. 1951.

34. This text will be found in Pierre Naville, *La Révolution et les intellectuels,* Gallimard, 1927, pp. 98–99. Naville does not indicate the signers, but they are mentioned, after an extract of the text, by Nadeau, *Histoire,* p. 107. Nadeau got the text from Raymond Queneau.

35. René Crevel, *L'Esprit contre la raison,* Cahiers du Sud, 1928.

36. *Entretiens,* p. 91.

37. *Ibid.,* p. 92.

38. *Ibid.,* p. 93.

39. *Ibid.*, p. 93.

40. *L'Amour fou*, p. 108.

41. See for example Michel Leiris, *L'Age d'homme*, Gallimard, 1939; and the beginning of *Aurora*, Gallimard, 1946. The extract from *L'Age d'homme* that Nadeau cites (*Histoire*, pp. 305–6) is particularly significant on this point.

42. Breton, *Anthologie de l'humour noir*, Sagittaire, 1950, p. 31.

43. *Les Pas perdus*, p. 83.

44. *Anthologie de l'humour noir*, pp. 141–42.

45. *Poisson soluble*, p. 85.

46. *Ibid.*, p. 77.

47. *Ibid.*, p. 83.

48. *Position politique du surréalisme*, p. 97.

49. See *Arts*, the number for 16 Nov. 1951.

50. *Ibid.*

51. *Arcane 17*, p. 25.

52. *Ibid.*, p. 22. Cf. "La Claire tour" (in *La Clé des champs*, pp. 271–74), where there is an unreserved eulogy on anarchism.

53. Both numbers are from 1925.

54. See *Point du jour*, p. 218.

55. See "Visite à Léon Trotsky," in *La Clé des champs*, pp. 42 ff.

56. Breton, *Ode à Charles Fourier*, Editions Fontaine, 1947.

57. *Arcane 17*, p. 23.

58. *Manifeste*, p. 9.

59. *Rupture inaugurale*. Editions surréalistes, June 1947, pp. 8–9. This fragment of text is by Henri Pastoureau; cf. "Pour une offensive de grand style contre la civilisation chrétienne," in *Le Surréalisme en 1947*, p. 81.

60. *La Révolution surréaliste*, no. 5, Oct. 1925. This manifesto was re-edited on the occasion of the Moroccan war.

61. Besides the members of these groups, the text was signed by Hermann Closson, Henri Jeanson, Pierre de Massot, Raymond Queneau, and Georges Ribemont-Dessaignes.

62. Pierre Naville, *La Révolution et les intellectuels*, p. 145.

63. These texts [by Artaud], published in the third number

of *La Révolution surréaliste,* are reprinted in Nadeau, *Documents surréalistes,* pp. 31–34.

64. Breton, "Légitime défense," in *La Révolution surrealiste* no. 8, Dec. 1926.

65. Maximilien Rubel, "Introduction à l'Ethique marxienne," in Karl Marx, *Pages choisies pour une éthique socialiste,* Marcel Rivière, 1948, p. xliv.

66. See the "Discours au congrès des écrivains" of June 1935, in *Position politique du surréalisme,* pp. 83–97.

67. See Dionys Mascolo, *Le Communisme,* Gallimard, 1953, pp. 230–35; and André Breton, "A la bonne heure," in *Médium,* Nov. 1953, p. 2.

68. *Position politique du surréalisme,* p. 11.

69. See *ibid.,* pp. 115–18.

70. See *La Clé des champs,* p. 267.

71. *Ibid.,* p. 268.

72. *Ibid.,* p. 269.

73. *Ibid.,* p. 271.

74. *Position politique du surréalisme,* p. 34.

75. *Ibid.,* p. 92.

76. *Ibid.,* p. 93.

77. *Ibid.,* pp. 23–24. On this problem, cf. Gaëtan Picon, *L'Ecrivain et son ombre,* Gallimard, 1953, pp. 143 ff.

78. *Ibid.,* p. 31.

79. *Ibid.,* p. 53.

80. Jean-Louis Bédouin, *André Breton,* p. 31.

81. *Ibid.,* p. 29.

82. Descartes, *Les Passions de l'âme,* art. 47.

83. Descartes, Letter to Balzac, 15 April 1631.

84. Breton, *Introduction au discours sur le peu de réalité,* Gallimard, 1927, p. 31. (Reprinted in *Point du jour,* p. 25.)

85. *Ibid.,* p. 32 (and in *Point du jour,* p. 26).

86. Rimbaud, *Une Saison en enfer,* Mauvais sang.

87. *La Révolution surréaliste,* no. 4, July 1925.

88. "Intellectio enim proprie mentis passio est." (Descartes to Regius, May 1641.)

89. *Introduction au discours sur le peu de réalité,* pp. 34–35 (in *Point du jour,* p. 29.)

90. *Poisson soluble,* pp. 100–101.

91. Gaston Bachelard, *L'Eau et les rêves*, José Corti, 1942, p. 203. [He is quoting Claudel's plans for a "subterranean church in Chicago."]
92. *Poisson soluble*, pp. 77–83.
93. Salvador Dali, "De la beauté terrifiante et comestible de l'architecture Modern'style," in *Minotaure*, nos. 3–4 (1933). [Dali is parodying the last sentence of Breton's *Nadja*: "Beauty will be convulsive or it will not be at all."]
94. See, for example, Salvador Dali, *La Conquête de l'irrationnel*, Editions Surréalistes, 1935, pl. 8.
95. See the reproductions of these objects in *Dictionnaire abrégé du surréalisme*, Galerie des Beaux-Arts, 1938, pp. 12–13 and 28.
96. *Les Pas perdus*, pp. 197–98.
97. See, for example, *Nadja*, p. 116.
98. *Position politique du surréalisme*, p. 125.
99. *Ibid.*, p. 138.
100. *Introduction au discours sur le peu de réalité*, pp. 27–28, and in *Point du jour*, p. 22.
101. See Breton, *Anthologie de l'humour noir*, Sagittaire, 1950, p. 189 ff.
102. *Ibid.*, p. 241.
103. *Ibid.*, pp. 319–20.
104. André Breton and Paul Eluard, *L'Immaculée conception*, Editions surréalistes, 1930, pp. 27–67.
105. *Ibid.*, p. 30.
106. *Ibid.*, p. 28.
107. *Entretiens*, p. 30. Cf. *Point du jour*, p. 70.
108. Julien Gracq, *Au Château d'Argol*, José Corti, n.d., p. 10.
109. *Nadja*, beginning. [The French equivalent for the expression, "He is known by the company he keeps," is "Dis-moi qui tu hantes et je te dirai qui tu es."]
110. *Anthologie de l'humour noir*, p. 14. ["Humour," in Freud, *Collected Papers*, V, 217.]
111. *Ibid.*, p. 9.
112. *Dictionnaire abrégé du surréalisme*, p. 14.
113. See this text in *Anthologie de l'humour noir*, pp. 109–11.
114. *Ibid.*, Jonathan Swift, "A Modest Proposal," pp. 22–27.
115. *Ibid.*, Alphonse Allais, "Plaisir d'été," pp. 183–87.

116. Julien Gracq, *André Breton,* p. 84. The phrase quoted and discussed by Gracq is from Monnerot, *La Poésie moderne et le sacré,* p. 95.

117. Breton, "Picasso dans son élément," in *Point du jour,* p. 197.

Chapter Three

1. *L'Amour fou,* pp. 122–23.

2. René Char, "L'Action de la justice est éteinte," in *Le Marteau sans maître,* José Corti, 1945, p. 27.

3. Paul Eluard, *L'Amour, la poésie,* Gallimard, 1929, p. 12.

4. Sarane Alexandrian finds the "ecstasy" of union with woman in what he calls "the carnal abandon." (See "Amour, révolte et poésie," in *Le Surréalisme en 1947,* p. 101.) But he speaks, perhaps without much logic, of the "face promising the infinite" of his loved one. Does he, then, love the face or the infinite it promises?

5. Aragon, *Le Paysan de Paris,* p. 157.

6. *Ibid.,* pp. 209–11.

7. *Ibid.,* p. 214.

8. Eluard, *Capitale de la douleur,* p. 55.

9. *Ibid.,* p. 140.

10. Paul Eluard, *Les Yeux fertiles,* G.L.M., 1936, p. 69.

11. *Capitale de la douleur,* p. 143.

12. *Nadja,* pp. 210–11.

13. See Paul Eluard, *Le Meilleur choix de poèmes est celui que l'on fait pour soi,* Sagittaire, 1947, pp. 11–12.

14. Eluard, "La Dame de carreau," in *Les Dessous d'une vie ou La Pyramide humaine,* 1926, reprinted in *Donner à voir,* Gallimard, 1939, p. 12.

15. Breton, "Enquête sur l'amour," in *La Révolution surréaliste,* no. 12, Dec. 1929.

16. *Ibid.*

17. As this of Eluard: "The hope of loving always, whatever happens to the being I love," *ibid.,* p. 71.

18. Text from the second edition of *Arcane 17,* reprinted in *Entretiens,* p. 140.

19. *L'Amour fou,* pp. 134–35.

20. See *Entretiens,* p. 140.

21. *L'Amour fou*, p. 135.
22. *Ibid.*, p. 112.
23. *Ibid.*, p. 172.
24. *Ibid.*, p. 171.
25. *L'Amour fou*, p. 9.
26. *Ibid.*, p. 11.
27. *Ibid.*, p. 12.
28. [Breton quotes this phrase from the end of Rimbaud's *Une Saison en enfer*.]
29. *Arcane 17*, p. 41. And in *Médium*, no. 4, Jan. 1955, Breton talks "of the necessity for the reconstitution of the primordial Androgyne" (p. 4.)
30. *Ibid.*, p. 35.
31. Eluard, *Les Yeux fertiles*, p. 57.
32. René Nelli, *L'Amour et les mythes du coeur*, Hachette, 1952, p. 140.
33. *Ibid.*, p. 144.
34. *Ibid.*, p. 145.
35. *Les Yeux fertiles*, p. 70.
36. *Arcane 17*, p. 96.
37. *Ibid.*, p. 72.
38. *Ibid.*, p. 80.
39. *Ibid.*, p. 135.
40. *Ibid.*, p. 40.
41. *Ibid.*, p. 138.
42. See *ibid.*, p. 92.
43. *Ibid.*, p. 96.
44. *Nadja*, p. 190.
45. *Les Yeux fertiles*, p. 75.
46. *Point du jour*, p. 75.
47. Robert Desnos, *Corps et biens*, Gallimard, 1930, p. 99.
48. *Ibid.*, p. 101.
49. *Arcane 17*, p. 176. Cf. *ibid.*, p. 83.
50. Baudelaire, "L'Invitation au voyage."
51. *Nadja*, pp. 7–8.
52. Eluard, "Toute ma vie t'écoute," in *Capitale de la douleur*, p. 140.
53. *Point du jour* p. 90.
54. *Ibid.*, p. 69.

55. Breton, "Avis au lecteur" for *La femme 100 têtes* of Max Ernst, reprinted in *Point du jour*, pp. 82–83.

56. *Manifeste*, p. 65.

57. Hugnet, *Petite anthologie poétique du surréalisme*, p. 151.

58. *Ibid.*, pp. 153–55.

59. In the Brussels magazine *Variétés*, June 1929, p. 10.

60. André Breton and Philippe Soupault, *Les Champs magnétiques*, Au Sans Pareil, 1921, "Barrières."

61. Aragon, *La Peinture au défi*, José Corti, Paris, 1930, p. 22.

62. *Ibid.*, p. 18.

63. *Ibid.*, pp. 14–15.

64. This "poetic anonymity," as Hugnet calls it, is particularly studied in *Ralentir travaux* (Editions Surréalistes, 1930), a collection of poems written in collaboration by Breton, Char, and Eluard.

65. *Les Pas perdus*, p. 246.

66. *Dictionnaire abrégé du surréalisme*, p. 9.

67. E. L. T. Mesens, "A Tort ou à raison," in *La Femme complète*, privately printed, 1933.

68. V. Raymond Polin, *La Création des valeurs*, P.U.F., 1946.

69. *Nadja*, p. 20.

70. *Ibid.*, p. 22.

71. *Ibid.*, p. 25.

72. *Ibid.*, p. 215.

73. *Ibid.*, p. 107.

74. *Ibid.*, pp. 115–16.

75. *Minotaure*, nos. 3–4, 1933, p. 102.

76. Joë Bousquet, *La Tisane de sarments*, Denoël et Steele, 1936, pp. 46–48.

77. *Nadja*, p. 24.

78. *Ibid.*, p. 23.

79. *Ibid.*

80. *L'Amour fou*, p. 58.

81. *Ibid.*, p. 59.

82. *Ibid.*, pp. 60–61.

83. Carrouges, *André Breton et les données fondamentales du surréalisme*, pp. 64 ff.

84. *Second manifeste,* p. 68.

85. *Ibid.,* p. 71.

86. *Ibid.,* p. 69.

87. *Ibid.,* p. 10.

88. Carrouges, *André Breton et les données fondamentales du surréalisme,* p. 24.

89. *Ibid.,* p. 20.

90. *Ibid.,* p. 30.

91. *Ibid.,* p. 24.

92. *L'Amour fou,* p. 171.

93. *Ibid.,* p. 129. Cf. *Les Vases communicants,* p. 109; *Entretiens,* p. 136.

94. "Enquête," *Minotaure,* nos. 3–4, p. 101.

95. *L'Amour fou,* p. 48.

96. *Ibid.,* p. 41.

97. *Nadja,* p. 33 and p. 56.

98. *Ibid.,* p. 108.

99. *Ibid.,* p. 113.

100. *Ibid.,* p. 148.

101. *Les Pas perdus,* p. 12.

102. Carrouges, *André Breton,* p. 61.

103. See *Nadja,* pp. 178 ff, *Point du jour,* pp. 115 ff.

104. See the text of the questionnaire on love, reprinted in *Entretiens,* p. 139. "Do you believe in the victory of admirable love over sordid life, or of sordid life over admirable love?"

105. P.-O. Lapie, "L'Insurrection surréaliste," *Cahiers du Sud,* Jan. 1935, p. 53.

106. Breton, *Les Vases communicants,* Cahiers Libres, 1932, pp. 101–102.

107. See Michel Carrouges, *La Mystique du surhomme,* Gallimard, 1948, Introduction.

108. Henri Pastoureau, "Pour une offensive de grand style contre la civilisation chrétienne," in *Le surréalisme en 1947,* pp. 78 ff.

109. Pastoureau, "Sade, précurseur d'une Weltanschauung de l'ambivalence," in *Almanach surréaliste du demi-siècle,* La Nef, 1950, pp. 39 ff.

110. René Char, Foreword to *Traduction d'Héraclite d'Ephèse* by Yves Battistini, Cahiers d'Art, 1948, pp. 12–13.

111. Pierre Berger, *René Char*, Seghers, 1951, p. 11.

112. Racine, *Bajazet*, Act II, scene 1.

113. Racine, *Hymnes traduites du bréviaire romain*, "Le Lundi à Laudes."

114. See Correspondence, *La Révolution surréaliste*, Dec. 1926, p. 26.

115. "Reverberate from the strident cry of red eggs." Benjamin Péret, "Tête à gifles," in *De Derrière les fagots*, Editions surréalistes, 1934, p. 17.

116. Edouard Maynial, *Anthologie des poètes du XIXe siècle*, Hachette, p. 268.

117. Etiemble, *Le Mythe de Rimbaud*, Gallimard.

118. Rimbaud, "Délires," I, *Une Saison en enfer*.

119. See *Entretiens*, p. 261.

120. Monnerot, *La poésie moderne et le sacré*, pp. 78 ff.

121. *Arcane 17*, pp. 153–54.

122. *Position politique du surréalisme*, p. 13.

123. *Situation du surréalisme entre les deux guerres*. See *La Clé des champs*, pp. 72–73. Cf. what Georges Bataille, in a different vein, says of "the absence of myth" in *Le Surréalisme en 1947*, p. 65.

124. See *Les Vases communicants*, pp. 33–73.

125. *Ibid.*, p. 63.

126. *Ibid.*, p. 128.

127. *Arcane 17*, p. 152.

128. *La Clé des champs*, p. 62.

129. *Ibid.*, p. 67.

130. *L'Amour fou*, p. 117.

131. *Nadja*, p. 74.

132. *Point du jour*, p. 40.

133. Marcel Raymond, *De Baudelaire au surréalisme*, José Corti, new edition, 1940, p. 12.

134. *Ibid.*, p. 15.

135. *L'Amour fou*, p. 75.

136. "Certain words carry with them representations that go past the physical representation. The Buttes-Chaumont raised in us a mirage. . . . All darkness was dissipated, under a hope immense and naive." *Le Paysan de Paris*, p. 165.

137. Reproduced in Hugnet, *Anthologie*, p. 97.

138. René Crevel, *Babylone,* Kra, 1927. Text cited in Hugnet, *ibid.,* p. 67.

139. *Arcane 17,* pp. 55–56. (I might state in passing that I am far from taking, as Breton does, the "revelations" of the theory of evolution for established truths.)

140. *Nadja,* p. 150.

Chapter Four

1. Paul Eluard, *Donner à voir,* Gallimard, 1939, p. 81.

2. *Second manifeste,* p. 9.

3. *Le Clé des champs,* p. 71.

4. *Point du jour,* p. 90.

5. *Ibid.,* p. 250.

6. *L'Amour fou,* p. 40.

7. *Les Vases communicants,* p. 102.

8. *Ibid.,* p. 122.

9. *Ibid.,* p. 99.

10. Eluard, *Donner à voir,* pp. 78–79.

11. *Ibid.,* p. 81.

12. The exact text of Breton is, "The imaginary is what tends to become real." See below.

13. Jacques Hérold, "L'Oeuf obéissant, l'oeuf désobéissant," in *Le Surréalisme en 1947,* p. 86.

14. See Breton, "Genèse et perspective artistiques du surréalisme," 1941, in *Le Surréalisme et la peinture,* Brentano's, 1946, p. 79; and Claude Mauriac, *André Breton,* p. 213.

15. Breton, *ibid.,* reproduced in *Yves Tanguy,* Pierre Matisse, New York, 1946, p. 30. Cf. Eluard, "Everything exists, everything is visible," in *La Rose publique,* Gallimard, 1934, p. 68.

16. Breton, "Il y aura une fois," in *Le Revolver à cheveux blancs,* p. 11.

17. *Manifeste,* p. 58.

18. *Les Vases communicants,* p. 50.

19. *Manifeste,* p. 35.

20. Thus, in his *Vocabulaire de psychologie,* Dugas cites, as type of the auditory image, the voices of Joan of Arc; as type of the visual image, the visions of Joan of Arc; as type of the gustatory image, the taste of arsenic Flaubert

had in his mouth for several days after describing the poisoning of Emma Bovary; as type of the olfactory image, the odor of hellish brimstone Ignatius of Loyola smelled while thinking about hell; as type of the tactile image, the example cited by Malebranche of a servant girl who, seeing her master's foot bleed, "felt such a pain at the same place on her foot that she was obliged to stay in bed three or four days afterward." For him, the essential character of the image is to be "hallucinatory." (V. L. Dugas, *Vocabulaire de psychologie,* Hachette, p. 69.) It is likely that the philosophy professors the surrealists knew while preparing their baccalaureats professed similar ideas on the image.

21. Breton, Introduction to an edition of the weird tales of Achim von Arnim, reprinted in *Point du jour,* pp. 167–69.

22. *Ibid.*

23. *Les Vases communicants,* p. 130.

24. *Ibid.,* pp. 123–24.

25. *Ibid.,* pp. 123–29.

26. *Point du jour,* pp. 250–51.

27. *Ibid.,* p. 224.

28. Salvador Dali, *La Conquête de l'irrationnel,* pp. 12–15.

29. Breton, "Le merveilleux contre le mystère," in *La Clé des champs,* p. 11.

30. On this contrast, see Yves Duplessis, *Le Surréalisme,* series "Que sais-je," P.U.F., 1950, p. 52.

31. *Point du jour,* pp. 226–27.

32. Dali, *La Conquête de l'irrationnel,* p. 17.

33. Cited by Breton, *Point du jour,* p. 219.

34. *Ibid.,* p. 171.

35. See René Nelli, *L'amour et les mythes du coeur,* p. 140.

36. "It may be that my life is merely an image of this kind," *Nadja,* p. 8.

37. "Eine verkörperte Traumwelt." See Christian Sénéchal, "Le Rêve chez les romantiques," in *Le Romantisme allemand,* special number of the *Cahiers du Sud,* May–June, 1937, pp. 86–88.

38. Albert Béguin, *Les Romantiques allemands et l'inconscient, ibid.,* p. 96.

39. "The peculiarity of the strong image is to have sprung from the bringing together of two quite distant realities,

whose relations only the spirit has grasped," and "The image is a pure creation of the spirit." Pierre Reverdy, *Le Gant de crin*, Plon, 1927, pp. 34 and 32.

40. *Les Vases communicants*, p. 129.

41. See *Le Revolver à cheveux blancs*, p. 67.

42. *L'Amour fou*, pp. 80 ff.

43. Breton, *Qu'est-ce que le surréalisme?* Henriquez, 1934.

44. Jean Brun, "Le Problème de la sensation et le surréalisme," in *Le Surréalisme en 1947*, p. 89.

45. On M. Pradines' conceptions of the imagination, see Maurice Pradines, *Traité de psychologie générale*, P.U.F., vols. 1 and 2.

46. *Position politique du surréalisme*, p. 37.

47. *Ibid.*

48. *La Clé des champs*, p. 71.

49. *Le Surréalisme et la peinture*, p. 94.

50. *Manifeste*, pp. 7–8.

51. *Le Surréalisme et la peinture*, pp. 43–44.

52. *La Clé des champs* (reprinting a text from *Point du jour*), p. 78.

53. Benjamin Péret, "La Demie de onze heures," in *Au 125 du boulevard Saint-Germain, Littérature*, 1923.

54. Notes added by Péret to his text "Les Parasites voyagent," in *Mort aux vaches et au champ d'honneur*. Cited, before publication, in Hugnet, *Anthologie*, pp. 121–22.

55. *Second manifeste*, p. 23.

56. *Manifeste*, p. 9.

57. *La Clé des champs*, p. 73.

58. *Arcane 17*, p. 29.

59. Gaëtan Picon, *L'Ecrivain et son ombre*, Gallimard, 1953, p. 124.

60. Emile Bouvier, *Initiation à la littérature d'aujourd'hui*, La Renaissance du Livre, 1927, pp. 198–200.

61. *L'Amour fou*, p. 26.

62. *Arcane 17*, pp. 32–34.

63. Gérard de Nerval, *Aurélia*, II, 6.

64. *Entretiens*, pp. 290–91.

65. *Ibid.*, p. 264.

66. *Ibid.*, p. 236.

67. "Love is to be rebuilt, like the rest." *Les Vases communicants,* p. 137.
68. *Entretiens,* p. 298.
69. *Position politique du surréalisme,* p. 34.
70. *Ibid.,* p. 132.
71. It is in this sense that Breton condemns what he calls the "error of Mallarmé," distrusts "completely external arrangements such as measure, rhythm, rhymes." (*Position politique du surréalisme,* pp. 136–37), denies that "the emancipation of style" can "consist in a laboratory exercise bearing abstractly on words," and is interested only in what he calls the "substance" of the work (*Point du jour,* pp. 52–53).
72. *Manifeste,* p. 24.
73. *Arcane 17,* pp. 24–25.
74. Monnerot, *La Poésie moderne et le sacré,* pp. 105–6.
75. *Ibid.,* p. 119.
76. *Ibid.,* p. 123.
77. *Entretiens,* p. 248.
78. *Manifeste,* pp. 19–22.
79. *L'Amour fou,* p. 7.
80. *Entretiens,* p. 248.
81. *Ibid.,* p. 258.
82. Victor Brauner, "Proclamation," in *Le Surréalisme en 1947,* p. 27.
83. Aragon, *Le Paysan de Paris,* p. 143.
84. *Ibid.,* p. 192.
85. *Ibid.,* p. 193.
86. *Ibid.,* p. 208.
87. *Ibid.,* p. 218.
88. *Ibid.,* p. 231.
89. E.g.: "Statue's honor, there isn't within a hundred thousand nooks of here one single activity, not even music-loving or Nicolas billiards, that seems to me as silly as psychology." *Ibid.,* p. 191.
90. *Ibid.,* p. 212.
91. *Ibid.,* p. 217.
92. Eluard, *L'Amour, la poésie,* p. 34.
93. Hugnet, *La Belle en dormant,* Cahiers libres, 1933. Cf. *Petite anthologie,* p. 103.

94. Breton, *L'Union libre* (1931), reprinted in Breton, *Poèmes*, Gallimard, 1948, pp. 65–67.

95. Monnerot, *La Poésie moderne et le sacré*, p. 168.

96. Max Ernst, "Comment on force l'inspiration," in *Le Surréalisme au service de la Révolution*, no. 6, p. 45.

97. *Point du jour*, pp. 220–21.

98. *Position politique du surréalisme*, pp. 164–65.

99. A reproduction of this work will be found in Hugnet, *Petite anthologie*, p. 144.

100. Breton, *Fata Morgana*, Editions des Lettres Françaises, Buenos-Aires, 1942; reprinted in *Poèmes*, Gallimard, p. 186.

101. Breton, "Signe ascendant," in *La Clé des champs*, p. 113.

102. *Ibid.*, p. 115.

103. *La Clé des champs*, p. 136.

104. *Les Vases communicants*, pp. 85–86.

105. See Gabriel Rey, *Humanisme et surhumanisme*, pp. 253 ff.

106. *Entretiens*, p. 266.

107. V. Nadeau, *Histoire du surréalisme*, p. 260: "On the level of this vital pessimism ... how ridiculous seem man, the world, God, life, and the multiple solutions of man to get out of his nightmare." Guy Dupré thinks "the vow of the black hermit of Croisset, to demoralize, has been fully satisfied by Breton" and speaks of the "malevolent powers" of Breton, whom he elsewhere admires profoundly (see "André Breton, le grand indésirable," in *Arts*, 29 Oct.–4 Nov. 1953). I believe, on the contrary, in surrealist optimism. But I am not sure that optimism and hope are, in surrealism, philosophically well founded.

108. *L'Amour fou*, p. 41.

109. *Entretiens*, p. 296. Contrasting science and art in that way, Breton refers to an article of Paalen, *Le Grand malentendu*.

110. *Les Vases communicants*, p. 164.

111. Such as the half-mask discovered by Giacometti and Breton at the flea market. See *L'Amour fou*, p. 44.

112. So, in an object constructed by Giacometti, "a ball of wood marked with a feminine crease is suspended by a fine violin string above a croissant with a fishbone from its cavity. The spectator finds himself instinctively forced

to make the ball glide over the fishbone, which the length of the string permits him to do only partly." *Le Surréalisme au service de la Révolution,* no. 3, p. 17. See in the same number a catalogue of surrealist objects, several texts devoted to these objects ("The culture of the spirit," Dali writes, "will be identified with the culture of desire"), and, at the end of the number, photographs of objects constructed by Giacometti, Valentine Hugo, André Breton, Gala Eluard, and Salvador Dali.

113. Baudelaire, *Les Fleurs du Mal,* Moesta et errabunda.

Postscript

1. *Entretiens,* p. 282. (Interview with José M. Valverde.)

2. Leon-Gabriel Gros, "Ta bouche aux lèvres d'or," *Cahiers du Sud,* no. 315, p. 191.

3. Paul Eluard and André Beaudin, *Doubles d'ombres,* Gallimard, 1945.

4. *Action,* number of Friday, 23 March 1945, p. 8. The title of the article is "Une Seule pensée." This is the title that Eluard had first given to his poem "Liberty."

5. I speak here only of the poems Eluard wrote under the occupation; they protest against injustice without proffering lies. The *Poèmes politiques* (Gallimard, 1948) and some lines of *Une Leçon de morale* (Gallimard, 1949) admittedly pose a different problem; sometimes here the poetic evidence is lost as well as, simply, the evidence. Often, however, the hope expressed remains universal. Even after 1945 it is mainly outside his written work that Eluard denied the surrealist ideal.

6. "Humanisme surréaliste et Humanisme existentialiste," in *L'Homme, le monde, l'histoire—Cahiers du collège philosophique,* 1948, p. 154.

7. *Entretiens,* p. 219.

8. This letter, in which in particular I manifested my indignation against the film *Road of Life,* had been published by Breton (with, of course, my full consent) in the fifth number of *Le Surréalisme au service de la Révolution.* See this number, p. 43, and *Entretiens,* p. 169.

9. *Entretiens,* pp. 219–20.

10. In a note on *Le Rendez-vous d'un soir d'hiver* by Joë Bousquet (René Debresse), which appeared in the Au-

gust number of the *Nouvelle Revue Française*, 1934, p. 305.

11. This text appeared in the *Journal des poètes* (Brussels), Jan. 1948.

12. It is in this sense that Marie-Josèphe Rustan rightly remarks that for Bousquet the absolute is "at once woof and horizon of things." See *Cahiers du Sud*, no. 320, p. 165.

13. *Nadja*, pp. 7–8.

14. This article appeared in the *Cahiers du Sud*, no. 303, pp. 187 ff.

15. "Confession spirituelle," in *Journal des poètes* (Brussels), Jan. 1948.

16. *Le Meneur de lune*, Janin, p. 14.

17. *Traduit du silence*, Gallimard, p. 9.

18. "Confession spirituelle," in *Journal des poètes* (Brussels), Jan. 1948.

19. *Le Poète de la connaissance du soir, ibid.*

20. *Le Meneur de lune*, p. 179.

21. *Traduit du silence*, p. 13.

22. *Le Meneur de lune*, p. 15.

23. *Le Passeur s'est endormi*, Denoël, p. 120.